guide

NATIONAL FOLK MUSEUM
THE NETHERLANDS OPEN-AIR MUSEUM

ARNHEM
1982

red route

short tour lasting

about one hour

This tour, which covers an area near the entrance, is mainly for people who are pressed for time and want a quick look round, but as there are no hills and a lot of seats along the way, it also a good route for older people and those unable to walk far.

It includes farmhouses from Staphorst, Zuid-Scharwoude, Giethoorn, Vierhouten and Harreveld; the sawmill and horse-driven oil mill; and the fisherman's cottage. It passes by the restaurant and through the "Zaan district", where the souvenir shop and special exhibitions building are situated, and a small detour can be made to the exhibition of costumes.

To get round in time it is probably advisable to limit detailed viewing to buildings marked with a ●

E Entrance
● 127 Small Achterhoek farmhouse *(los hoes)* - Harreveld (Gld.)
● 22 Farmhouse - Staphorst (Ov.)
● 32 Farmhouse with pyramid roof - Zuid-Scharwoude (N.H.)
33 Double drawbridge - Ouderkerk on the Amstel (N.H.)
● 34 Merchant's house - Koog on the Zaan (N.H.)
35 Souvenir shop (S) and Exhibition (EX)

● 41 Building for temporary exhibitions
42 Boatyard - Marken (N.H.)
● 43 Fisherman's cottage - Marken (N.H.)
44 Sheepcote - Texel (N.H.)
45 Small drainage mill (fantail type) - Gouda (Z.H.)
46 Eelmonger's hut - Amsterdam (N.H.)
47 Sawmill - Numansdorp (Z.H.)
23 Large farmhouse - Oud-Beijerland (Z.H.)
● 24 Farmhouse - Giethoorn (Ov.)

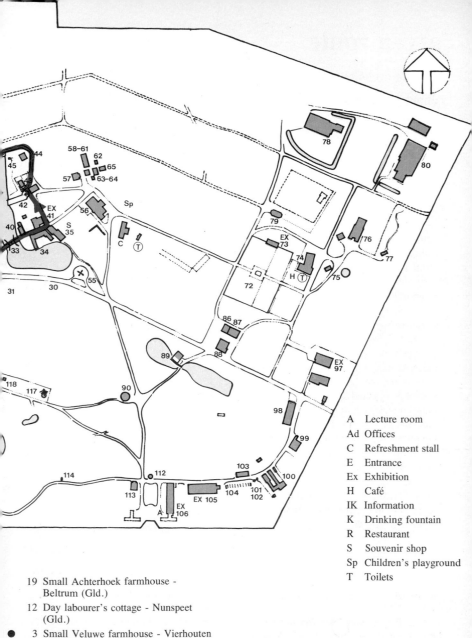

A   Lecture room
Ad   Offices
C   Refreshment stall
E   Entrance
Ex   Exhibition
H   Café
IK   Information
K   Drinking fountain
R   Restaurant
S   Souvenir shop
Sp   Children's playground
T   Toilets

19 Small Achterhoek farmhouse -
    Beltrum (Gld.)

12 Day labourer's cottage - Nunspeet
    (Gld.)

● 3 Small Veluwe farmhouse - Vierhouten
    (Gld.)

● 1 Horse-driven oil mill - Zieuwent
    (Gld.)

● 125 Exhibition of costumes

green route

medium-length tour lasting

about two hours

This tour is for the average visitor with a general interest and for school parties and other groups. It takes at least two hours, covering a large area of the museum, with a good cross-section of the exhibits, from farmhouses to mills and rural trades and industries.

It includes farmhouses from Vierhouten, Varik, Staphorst and Zuid-Scharwoude; the horse-driven oil mill, polder drainage mill, sawmill, post mill and paper mill; the wheelwright's shop and boatyard; as well as the fisherman's cottage, the Hindeloopen parlour and the "Zaan district", where the souvenir shop and special exhibitions building are situated. It passes by the restaurant, the café at the "Hanekamp" inn, and the refreshment stall for school parties (C), and small detours can be made to the exhibition of costumes and to three more exhibitions.

To get round in time, it is probably advisable to limit detailed viewing to buildings marked with a ●

E Entrance
- ● 1 Horse-driven oil mill - Zieuwent (Gld.)
- 2 Fowler's hut - Aerdenhout (N.H.)
- ● 3 Small Veluwe farmhouse - Vierhouten (N.H.)
- 4 Exhibition of bee-keeping
- ● 5 Betuwe farmhouse - Varik (Gld.)
- 11 Pebble floor - Geesteren (Gld.)
- 12 Day labourer's cottage - Nunspeet (Gld.)
- 13 Sheepcote - Ederveen (Gld.)

- 19 Small Achterhoek farmhouse - Beltrum (Gld.)
- ● 22 Farmhouse - Staphorst (Ov.)
- ● 32 Farmhouse with pyramid roof - Zuid-Scharwoude (N.H.)
- 48 Drainage mill - Noordlaren (Gr.)
- 47 Sawmill - Numansdorp (Z.H.)
- 46 Eelmonger's hut - Amsterdam (Z.H.)
- 45 Small drainage mill (fantail type) - Gouda (Z.H.)
- 44 Sheepcote - Texel (N.H.)
- ● 43 Fisherman's cottage - Marken (N.H.)

4

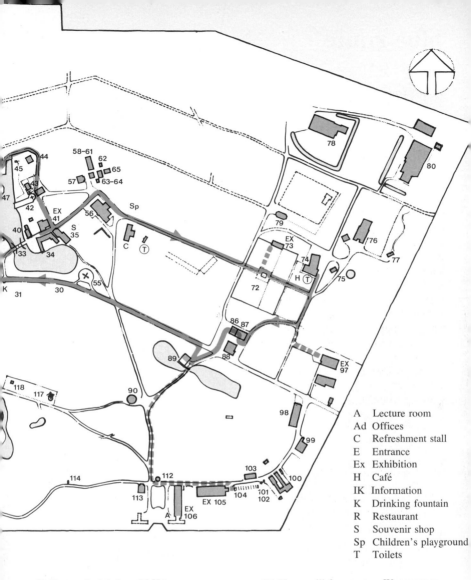

A   Lecture room
Ad Offices
C   Refreshment stall
E   Entrance
Ex Exhibition
H   Café
IK Information
K   Drinking fountain
R   Restaurant
S   Souvenir shop
Sp Children's playground
T   Toilets

42 Boatyard - Marken (N.H.)

● 41 Building for temporary exhibitions

35 Souvenir shop (S) and exhibition (EX)

34 Merchant's house - Koog on the Zaan (N.H.)

56 Laundry - Overveen (N.H.)

C Refreshment stall

● 72 Herb garden

73 Herb garden exhibition building

● 74 Farmhouse-inn, "De Hanekamp" - Zwolle (Ov.)

87 Horse mill for groats – Wormerveer (N.H.)

● 86 Parlour - Hindeloopen (Fr.)

● 89 Paper mill - Veluwe (Gld.)

55 Post mill - Huizen (N.H.)

● 127 Small Achterhoek farmhouse (*los hoes*) - Harreveld (Gld.)

128 Achterhoek wheelwright's shop - Woold (Gld.)

R Restaurant

● 125 Exhibition of regional costumes

5

blue route

long tour lasting

about four hours

This tour covers the whole museum and is meant for people who come for the day or have at least four hours to spare. It can easily be broken half way, for refreshments (or a meal) at the restaurant or a drink at the café in the "Hanekamp" inn.

It takes in all the major farmsteads, houses, mills and workshops, as well as the herb garden, the exhibition of costumes, the exhibition of farm carts and other vehicles, and the "Zaan district", where the souvenir shop and special exhibitions building are situated.

To get round in time, it is probably advisable, even here, to limit detailed viewing to buildings marked with a ●

    E Entrance
    R Restaurant

● 125 Exhibition of costumes
● 115 Small Twente farmhouse (*los hoes*) - Beuningen (Ov.)
  113 Toll collector's house - Zuidlaren (Dr.)
  106 Lecture room and exhibition
● 105 Exhibition
  104 Archery butts - Roermond (L.)
  103 South Limburg outhouse - Terstraeten (L.)
  101 Limburg wayside shrine - Margraten (L.)
● 100 South Limburg farmstead - Krawinkel (L.)
   99 Brewery and bakehouse - Ulvenhout (N.Br.)
   98 Kempen farmhouse - Budel (N.Br.)
   97 Farmstead - Etten en Leur (N.Br.)
● 74 Farmhouse-inn, "De Hanekamp" - Zwolle (Ov.)
   75 Village school - Lhee (Dr.)
● 76 Drenthe farmhouse (*los hoes*) - Zeijen (Dr.)

   77 Day labourer's cabin - Onstwedde (Gr.)
● 78 Frisian farmstead - Midlum (Fr.)
   73 Herb garden exhibition building
● 72 Herb garden
● 80 Groningen farmstead - Beerta (Gr.)
● 86 Parlour - Hindeloopen (Fr.)
   87 Horse mill for groats - Wormerveer (N.H.)
● 89 Paper mill - Veluwe (Gld.)
   55 Post mill - Huizen (N.H.)
   56 Laundry - Overveen (N.H.)
57-65 Cottage, workman's terrace houses, clogmaker's workshop and shoeing-shed
● 43 Fisherman's cottage - Marken (N.H.)

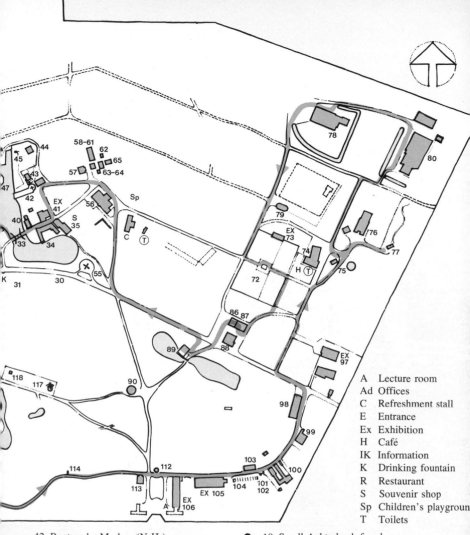

A   Lecture room
Ad Offices
C   Refreshment stall
E   Entrance
Ex Exhibition
H   Café
IK Information
K   Drinking fountain
R   Restaurant
S   Souvenir shop
Sp Children's playground
T   Toilets

42 Boatyard - Marken (N.H.)
● 41 Building for temporary exhibitions
35 Souvenir shop (S) and exhibition
● 34 Merchant's house -
Koog on the Zaan (N.H.)
33 Double drawbridge - Ouderkerk on the
Amstel (N.H.)
48 Drainage mill - Noordlaren (Gr.)
● 47 Sawmill - Numansdorp (Z.H.)
23 Large farmhouse - Oud-Beijerland
(Z.H.)
● 32 Farmhouse with pyramid roof -
Zuid Scharwoude (N.H.)
● 22 Farmhouse - Staphorst (Ov.)
21 Dovecote - Hamersveld (Utr.)
20 Farmhouse from the Vollenhove
district - Kadoelen (Ov.)

● 19 Small Achterhoek farmhouse -
Beltrum (Gld.)
13 Sheepcote - Ederveen (Gld.)
12 Day labourer's cottage - Nunspeet
(Gld.)
11 Pebble floor - Geesteren (Gld.)
● 5 Betuwe farmhouse - Varik (Gld.)
4 Exhibition of bee-keeping
● 3 Small Veluwe farmhouse - Vierhouten
(Gld.)
2 Fowler's hut - Aerdenhout (N.H.)
● 1 Horse-driven oil mill -
Zieuwent (Gld.)
128 Achterhoek wheelwright's shop
Woold (Gld.)
● 127 Small Achterhoek farmhouse - (los
hoes) - Harreveld (Gld.)

7

Foreword

The Netherlands Open-Air Museum, founded in 1912
tries to present a picture of the daily life of ordinary
people in this country as it was in the past and has
developed in the course of time. This is done mainly
by means of old buildings such as farmhouses, barns,
workshops and mills, with all the furnishings and
equipment appurtaining to them; but it is the people
who lived and worked in them who are important. In
compiling this guide, therefore, we have concentrated
on the social and economic background rather than
overburdening the visitor with technical terms or local
names, or giving detailed accounts of the past history
of the buildings, which in any case have mostly found
their way to the museum more or less by chance.
On the next few pages all the buildings and other
major objects are listed in numerical order and briefly
described. The rest of the guide is devoted to a more
thorough discussion of certain aspects, and here
selected buildings are arranged in a logical sequence,
with the links between them being emphasised by
means of cross-references, which also help to avoid
repetition.
It is obviously impossible to cover all the objects
inside the buildings, but as visitors often want to know
how old things are, some general indication of this has
been given where it seemed appropriate. Dates are
seldom found on the sort of objects shown here and it
is usually impossible to date them precisely. In fact
most of the buildings contain a mixture of things,
some dating from around 1900, others earlier.
In a general guide like this footnotes and a
bibliography seem out of place and have therefore
been dispensed with, but anyone wishing for further
information may apply to the museum library or the
department dealing with documentation.

The Director and Staff
of the Netherlands Open-Air Museum

Brief descriptions in numerical order

1 **HORSE-DRIVEN OIL MILL FROM ZIEUWENT (Gld.)** p. 92
Mill for pressing oil from seeds. Installed in the barn at the back of a farmhouse about 1830.

2 **FOWLER'S HUT FROM AERDENHOUT (N.H.)**
Hut dating shortly before 1900. Tackle for catching small birds can be seen inside. Trapping finches by luring them into large nets used to be a favourite pastime of the well-to-do.

3 **SMALL VELUWE FARMHOUSE FROM VIERHOUTEN (Gld.)** p. 43
Small farm from an area with poor sandy soil. Built about 1850. Really more like a farm labourer's cottage.

4 **EHIBITION OF BEEKEEPING**
Exhibition of traditional and modern hives and other equipment used in beekeeping. In the past honey was used as sweetener in much the same way as sugar nowadays.

5 **BETUWE FARMHOUSE FROM VARIK (Gld.)** p. 51
Basic structure dating from 1646, with later additions and alterations, presenting a typical picture of a farm in the Betuwe area at the end of the nineteenth century.

6-10 Reserve numbers for future acquisitions.

11 PEBBLE FLOOR FROM GEESTEREN (Gld.)
Floors like this were common in farm kitchens in the Achterhoek region of Gelderland (see No. 127, and also No. 19).
This particular example (roofed over for protection) was
originally laid in 1838 and incorporates the initials of subsequent inhabitants of the farm.

12 DAY LABOURER'S COTTAGE FROM p. 47
NUNSPEET (Gld.)
Small one-roomed cottage with tiny barn behind, from the
second half of the nineteenth century. Type lived in by casual
labourers on the Veluwe heathland.

13 SHEEPCOTE FROM EDERVEEN (Gld.) p. 50
Shelter for at night. Type common until about 1900.

14-18 Reserve numbers for future acquisitions.

19 SMALL ACHTERHOEK FARMHOUSE p. 38
FROM BELTRUM (Gld.)
Farm with weaving as a cottage industry. Basic structure
dating from about 1750, with alterations carried out before
1850.

20 FARMHOUSE FROM KADOELEN IN THE p. 62
VOLLENHOVE DISTRICT (Ov.)
Built about 1800, with subsequent alterations. Mainly cattle.

21 DOVECOTE FROM HAMERSVELD (Utr.)
The doves were kept as pets and were sometimes also eaten.

59-62 WORKMEN'S TERRACE HOUSES FROM TILBURG (N.Br.)

These houses, which are about a hundred years old, are typical of the working-class dwellings in the towns of Brabant. *Not open to visitors.*

62 CLOGMAKER'S WORKSHOP   p. 41

Small outhouse containing the tools and equipment used in clogmaking.

63 WORKMAN'S COTTAGE FROM ZANDEWEER (Gr.)

This cottage, dating from c. 1850, is now used as a smithy for the restoration and upkeep of objects in the museum.

64 SHOEING-SHED FROM SCHERPENZEEL (Gld.)

Tethering the horse between the posts of this shed made shoeing easier.

65 FARM LABOURER'S COTTAGE FROM BEEMSTER (N.H.)

Not open to visitors.

66-71 Reserve numbers for future acquisitions.

72 HERB GARDEN   p. 116

In this garden numerous old medicinal herbs and other plants are grown. The two monumental gates, from old country houses, and the stone pump, from Zwolle, are all about 250 years old.

112 SUMMER-HOUSE FROM MEPPEL (Dr.)
Copy of a summer-house of c. 1840. The original is still to be
seen in Meppel. Well-to-do people often had summer-houses
in their gardens, near the water's edge if possible. In fine
weather they would spend a lot of time in them, drinking tea
and so on. *Not open to visitors.*

113 TOLL COLLECTOR'S HOUSE FROM   p. 88
ZUIDLAREN (Dr.)
Toll-gate and house of c. 1850.

114 BOUNDARY POST OF A HUNTING
GROUND FROM ARNHEM (Gld.)
The limits of a hunting ground were generally marked with
posts like this one, which dates from the nineteenth century
and comes from the former manor of Meijnerswijk to the
south of Arnhem.

115 SMALL TWENTE FARMHOUSE FROM   p. 30
BEUNINGEN (Ov.)
Small farm (*los hoes*) without a dividing wall between barn
and house place. Built c. 1700.

116 TWENTE BAKEHOUSE FROM   p. 33
DENEKAMP (Ov.)
Small building of 1741 containing a bread-oven.

117 SMALL DRAINAGE MILL FROM   p. 109
WOUTERSWOUDE (Fr.)
Small mill with screw pump used for draining meadows.
Dates from c. 1870.

118 SMALL DRAINAGE MILL FROM   p. 110
GORREDIJK (Fr.)
Nineteenth-century hollow post mill for draining meadows.

119-124 Reserve numbers for future acquisitions.

125 EXHIBITION OF COSTUMES
The exhibition, which is changed from time to time,
comprises material from the museum's own collection. Gui-
des are on sale at the entrance to the building.

126 SHED FOR DRYING WOOD FROM   p. 107
HAARLEM (N.H.)
Built c. 1850. *Not open to visitors.*

127 SMALL ACHTERHOEK FARMHOUSE   p. 35
FROM HARREVELD (Gld.)
Small farm (*los hoes*), with some cottage industry. Goes back
to c. 1770.

128 ACHTERHOEK WHEELWRIGHTS'S SHOP   p. 40
FROM WOOLD (Gld.)
Here can be seen the tools used in making wheels for carts and
wagons, a craft carried on as a cottage industry until around
1900.

SOUTH LIMBURG OUTHOUSE
FROM TERSTRAETEN (L.)

■ This outhouse, built about 1800, is a good example of a *timber-framed construction*, with walls filled in with *wattle and daub*. Inside are presses, tubs and pans for making syrup from apples and pears. This used to be a common rural industry in South Limburg, a traditional fruit-growing area.

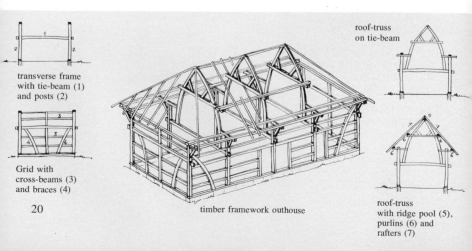

transverse frame with tie-beam (1) and posts (2)

Grid with cross-beams (3) and braces (4)

timber framework outhouse

roof-truss on tie-beam

roof-truss with ridge pool (5), purlins (6) and rafters (7)

☐ Frame structures are still very much a feature of modern building. Nowadays steel and reinforced concrete are mostly used, but for centuries the load-bearing framework of houses, barns and sheds was made of wood, fashioned by the local carpenter, or wright. The framework of this particular building, clearly visible both inside and out, gives a good idea of how it was done.

First, a series of *transverse frames* were constructed, each consisting of two stout poles joined by a tie-beam anchored on the outside with wooden pegs. (In this building there are five such frames.) These were then hoisted, or "reared", into an upright position, one behind the other, and made firm round the outer walls by means of crossbeams and braces, to form the familiar grid pattern in which door and window frames were completely integrated.

On the tie-beams, *roof-trusses* were mounted (though the end-trusses were sometimes omitted, as in this case). To make these, conveniently curved trunks or branches were sawn lengthwise with a long two-handed saw, so as to produce two symmetrical timbers like those used in shipbuilding. Once in position, the trusses were tied by a ridge pole and purlins, to which rafters were fastened with wooden pegs. The rafters were then covered with thatch, or laths and tiles, as required.

Such a construction, basically a *simple nave without aisles* was common in South Limburg.

The filling-in of the walls with wattle was carried out by springing upright laths into grooves notched in the crosstimbers, and cross-weaving them with twigs or brushwood to form a close hurdling. The whole family, with their friends, would then probably lend a hand smearing the wattle with layers of daub, which consisted of a pulp of clay, chopped straw and cow-dung. Different recipes, of course, were used at different times and there were variations from district to district, but when finished, the cellular structures of such a wall, with its numerous pockets of air, would provide excellent insulation, well protected against the elements by the overhanging eaves.

The wooden locks on the two left-hand doors would seem to be prototypes of the modern Yale lock. In fact, locks like this used to be quite common all over the world, which only goes to prove there is virtually nothing new under the sun.

cross-section through wattle and daub

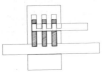

wattle hurdling

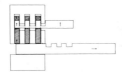

bolt locked

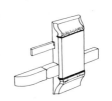

bolt withdrawn

wooden lock

SOUTH LIMBURG FARMSTEAD 100
FROM KRAWINKEL (L.)

■ This farm, and many others like it in South Limburg, will probably have started as a cottage attached to a smallholding and taken a hundred years or more to expand into the huddled complex of buildings and backyards which we find here. Important dates in its development are recorded over the doors and in the stonework round the window at the front. The latest addition, the pigsty, is probably not much more than a hundred years old. The farming will have been mixed, with orchards, arable and rich riverside pastures, but all on a fairly modest scale.

keystone

brickwork panelling

lintel

Crucifix

bench

wooden bench

☐ Most of the buildings here are based on a simple aisleless framework like that in No. 103 (p. 21), but many of the wattle-and-daub panels have been redone with bricks. As bricks became cheaper, or the farmer more prosperous, this seem to have been a fairly common practice when a farm needed renovating, especially on the higher ground in the east of the country and in South Limburg. In the present instance, even part of the timber frame has been replaced by brickwork.

Brick, of course, had always been much more respectable than wattle and daub, and in the eighteenth and nineteenth centuries many an old wattle-and-daub building was given a brick façade, thereby altering the character of numerous village streets in South Limburg where the rows of brick-fronted farms became a very distinctive feature. Behind the smart façade, however, the old huddle of buildings, lean-tos and sheds remained unaltered.

Thus, from the street, this farm would appear to be a broad, brick-built affair. But on passing through the gate on the right we find a long, rather narrow timber-framed house with a series of outhouses. In the farmhouse itself, the room at the front used to be the "best room", reserved for special occassions. It has clayplastered walls and ceiling and is furnished in the style fashionable at the beginning of this century. From here a small doorway opens into the kitchen, with its open fireplace, which was where the family normally lived.

Leading off the kitchen is a small bedroom with a cupboard bed, and beyond this the back-kitchen and cellar where, among other things, the milk from the goats and the farm's small herd of cows was made into butter for sale in the neighbouring town. The usual earthenware vessels are stacked in the cupboard. There is also a bench of the type that was once quite common in simple dwellings but tended to persist in South Limburg longer than anywhere else. The brick fireplace was used to boil up fodder which was then taken out to the sheds on a small trolley.

The back-kitchen looks out across the main farmyard (with its dung heap) to the privy, pigsties, stables, byres and barns for storing hay and the harvest. On the other side of the house is another yard, for the cart; at the front there is a covered well, and at the back a bakehouse for baking bread and pastry.

A farm of this size will usually have provided the farmer and his family with little more than a bare subsistence, which they will have been compelled to eke out with money earned as labourers on the other farms and as seasonal workers in quarries across the border, or from weaving and making simple wrought ironwork for the German market.

trolley

DRENTHE FARMHOUSE FROM ZEIJEN (Dr.)   76

■ Up to about the beginning of this century, this type of farmhouse was common along the sandy ridges stretching southwards from the south-east corner of Groningen to the eastern (Achterhoek) region of Gelderland. Known locally as a *los hoes*, it is characterized by the absence of a dividing wall between the house place (*i.e.* the farm kitchen and its hearth) and the barn: men and beasts lived together in one large communal area. This particular example from Drenthe has an *aisle on either side of the central nave* and both inside and outside walls are filled in with wattle and daub. The furnishings and fitments, in the style of a large *los hoes* of around 1700, are based on material found during the demolition of a farmhouse in Zeijen, near Assen.

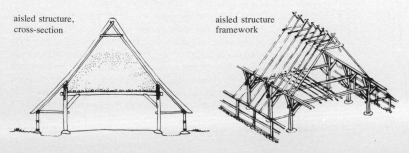

aisled structure, cross-section

aisled structure framework

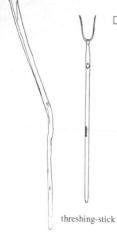

threshing-stick

pitchfork

flail

☐ Compared with No. 103 (p. 20), the only differences in construction are the addition of the aisles, formed by bringing the roof down beyond the posts, and the omission of the cumbersome curved-tree roof-trusses. The result was a highly compact and efficient design, since the low aisles were quite high enough for stalls, while the tall nave would easily take a fully laden farmcart as well as allow for the swinging of flails and sticks when the barn floor was being used as a threshing-floor (see Fig. p. 119). The removal of the curved-tree trusses also meant that there was now more storage space in the loft above the beams, which was important because threshing was only done as and when the grain was required, thereby making it necessary to store the harvest for some time in sheaves.

On entering the barn, which faces the road at the front of the building, we find ourselves on the broad, mud *threshing-floor*, with the loft above, and in the aisle on the right the *sunken stall* for the fifteen to twenty head of cattle that would have been kept on a farm of this size. "Stall" is perhaps a euphemism, as it is really little more than a pit dug in the ground. But, like the other parts of the building, it served its purpose very effectively, allowing the farmer simply to strew the cow-dung with layers of chopped straw and turf, until eventually the animals stood on a level with the floor of the barn. It would then be cleaned out and the manure would be used to enrich the arable land on which the rye, buckwheat and other cereals were grown.

The manure, in fact, was the main reason for keeping cows on a farm like this, and the same could often be said of sheep, especially in Drenthe. Unlike cows, however, which consumed some of the farm's cereal produce, sheep were quite content with what they could find on the surrounding heathland, and all that was needed to collect their droppings was to drive them into pens every night. Also, some of the wool they provided could be sold, and some could be spun into yarn to weave cloth for the family's own use.

Indeed, much of what the farm produced went to satisfy the

26

household's own needs, which were quite considerable. Besides wool for clothes, rye was needed to bake bread and quite a sizeable proportion of the produce went as payment in kind to the farm labourers and the craftsmen that had to be called in from time to time. Even so, a large farm like this would usually still have quite a good surplus of grain and wool, which would be sold, often outside the district, to provide money for various "luxuries" as well as a little capital to put by for hard times or to invest in equipment or perhaps a horse. (Horse trading and rearing were very important in Drenthe.)

skep

A writer at the beginning of the nineteenth century, commenting on the *los hoes*, pointed out that the great advantage of this centuries-old method of building was that the woman of the house could sit at her spinning-wheel, keeping an eye not only on the fire, the food in the pot and the baby in the cradle, but also on all the livestock as well as the rest of the family at work in the barn, and could issue her orders without stirring from her chair. Nowadays, however, it is thought that another important reason for this type of design was that the smoke rising freely from the open fire was an excellent means of drying and preserving the harvest stored in the loft.

reel

The land in Drenthe – old and well established though it was – was only partly cultivated and the few villages that there were, scattered about the landscape, were fairly small, just a few large farms clustered round a tree-lined green (usually with a pond in the middle) and here and there houses belonging to less well-off small-holders, labourers and village craftsmen. These smaller houses were generally more or less scaled-down versions of the large farmhouses, and although their inhabitants usually had a small piece of land and a few head of cattle, this was not sufficient to live off. Instead they bartered their labour, services and produce for food and the use of capital goods which they could not afford themselves, but which the larger farmers could provide, like horses, ploughs and farm wagons. As a result, the large farmer, smallholder (hardly distinguishable from the farm labourer) and craftsman, bound by their dependence on one another, came to form a close-knit community in which people lived frugally but generally managed to ward off impoverishment.

hackle

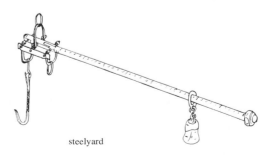

steelyard

VILLAGE SCHOOL FROM LHEE (Dr.)

■ This small, rectangular brick building probably dates from shortly before 1750. It rests on a foundation of cobbles and the floor inside is also made of cobbles, as in the living area of many farmhouses. In the centre there is an open hearth under a wooden hood. The interior has been arranged to give some idea of what a country school was like and what sort of things would be used in it in the early nineteenth century (1800–30).

satchel

☐ The strong sense of community found amongst the people of Drenthe (see p. 27) was not only directed towards solving problems specifically connected with farming: more than one village school like this owed its existence to the initiative of local farmers.

Like the shepherd, the teacher was in the service of the community and took his meals with the various farmers turn and turn about. He was, however, a sort of seasonal worker, as there was no school in summer when the children had to help on the land. His salary was minimal and he would have to supplement it by seling such requisites of learning as quill pens, ink, paper and so on. He might also act as sexton or perform some other service such as winding the church clock every day. It was his pupils who supplied the fuel (peat, turves, etc.) for the fire. Needless to say, the education he dispensed was not of a very high order, being largely confined to the three R's and religious instruction.

ferule

disgrace mark

SMALL TWENTE FARMHOUSE   115
FROM BEUNINGEN (Ov.)

■ This little *los hoes* (p. 25), which comes from the eastern part of the province of Overijssel known as Twente, was built about 1700. It has half-timbered walls filled with wattle and daub (p. 21) and oakplanked gables patterned with straw thatch. Details of how a farmhouse of this type was run are given on p. 26-27.

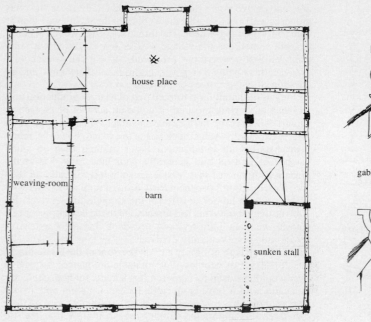

house place

weaving-room

barn

sunken stall

gable finials

kettle

fireguard

☐ As in Drenthe the older farms in Twente are settled on the sandy soils found on the higher ground. Instead of being grouped together in villages, however, the farmhouses here were often scattered about the countryside, separated from their neighbours by woods and wasteland. They were usually quite large structures of the *los hoes* type and would have various smaller buildings nearby: a sheepcote, a bakehouse for breadmaking (p. 33), perhaps a small water-mill and very often, at a later period, a cartshed. There might also have been a smaller *los hoes* , like this one, meant for elderly parents or for a farm labourer who was allowed to cultivate a small patch of land on his own account.

The economy of such a tiny farm was modest indeed. Each year a small plot was given over to the rye from which people made their own bread; a goat was kept for milk, a pig and a couple of sheep for meat and wool, and in the sunken stall in the aisle (p.

well

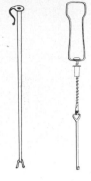

blowpipe   pot-hanger

cooking-pot

spinning-wheel

hand churn

26), one or two cows for their dung. Generally some flax was grown as well and this, like the wool from the sheep, was spun at home on a spinning-wheel. The thread was often woven at home too, but sometimes the village weaver was entrusted with this task. Virtually everything produced was for the household's own use, there being no significant surpluses of any kind, and no question of using horses or building up reserves.

As long as the small farm formed part of a larger production unit its inhabitants were ensured of a certain amount of protection against penury, crop failures and suchlike. When the population of Twente and the Achterhoek began to expand, however, many people started up independent farms of their own on small patches of unused and generally poor land, and due to the precarious nature of their existence soon lost virtually all they had, thereby giving rise to an early form of rural proletariat with nothing but its labour to offer in the struggle for survival. By 1700 or thereabouts this had already led to the development of a cottage weaving industry, out of which Twente's extensive textile industry eventually evolved.

The fireplace here is simply a pit in the floor of the house place, which is made of pebbles. The rotatable pot-hanger suspended over it could be used to support either a kettle for household use or a cauldron for boiling up cattle fodder. Cooking-pots would be placed on a trivet (drawing on p. 36) or simply stood on their own three legs among the glowing ashes. At night-time the fire was sometimes the only source of light, though it might be supplemented by a small oil- or fat-lamp. When people went to bed, it was damped down with turves and covered with a wrought-iron guard, and in the morning it was blown up again with an iron blowpipe or a pair of bellows. In the absence of a chimney the smoke had to find its own way out through cracks and crannies. The inhabitants slept on straw in the rough wooden cupboard beds in the aisles. They had to get their water from the well outside, using a counterbalanced beam to raise the bucket.

■ This bakehouse once stood near a large Twente *los hoes* .
The date 1741 is carved over the door. Bakehouses were
often built separately from the farmhouse because of the
risk of fire. Most of the other examples in the museum
simply consist of the bread-oven with a little roof over it,
but this one is quite a large affair in which the oven
occupies only a small part.

The oven is essentially a small chamber made of bricks
and clay. This would be heated by lighting a fire of
faggots inside, the mouth being left open to let the moke
out. When the bricks were hot enough, the fire would be
raked out and the risen dough pushed inside with the aid of
a peel. The oven would then be closed and the dough
would bake in the heat retained by the bricks. Under the
shelter by the side of this bakehouse bees were kept.

lintel

peel

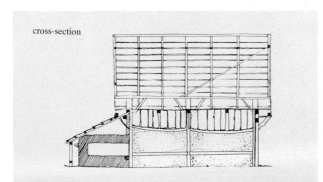

cross-section

dough trough

33

■ The earliest record we have of this farm, which again is an aisled *los hoes* (p. 25), dates from 1771 and the oldest parts of the building could also date from that period. When it was transferred to the museum, however, both exterior and interior were kept as they were found, in the form they had assumed in the course of the nineteenth century. Only the front wall is still done in wattle and daub, all the other outside walls being brick. The blue wash over the daub and on the clay walls inside was customary in this area, perhaps as a means of warding off flies.

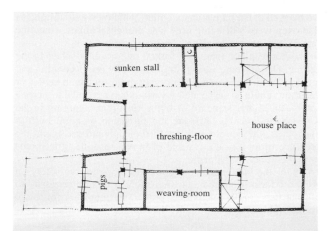

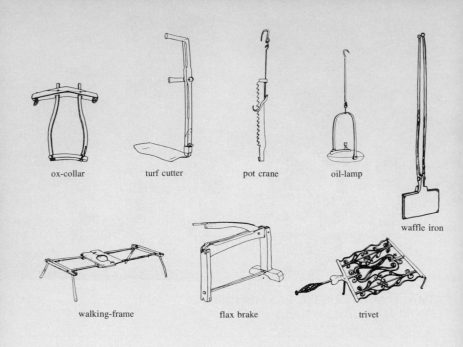

ox-collar   turf cutter   pot crane   oil-lamp   waffle iron

walking-frame   flax brake   trivet

☐ The scale and organization of the work on this little farm would
have been much the same as described on p. 30, except that the
stall for the cows is slightly larger (capable of taking three or five
animals) and there is also a pigsty. To accommodate these the
building has been extended at the back, past the last posts of the
timber frame (p. 20). During the course of the nineteenth century, animal husbandry came to take pride of place in the agriculture of the sandy soils in the eastern part of the country, with the
result that arable farming was reduced to little more than the
minimum necessary to feed the stock. By 1870 local markets had
virtually ceased to handle field crops and were mainly devoted to
such animal products as were in excess of the farmers' own
needs.

On the wall of the barn is an ox-collar, which serves to remind us
that oxen were still being used was draught animals, since the
farmer was unable to afford the luxury of a horse.

In the house place there is a forked tree-trunk attached to the
ceiling. On this hang various implements for use in cooking and
tending the fire, including an iron pot crane on which kettles or
cauldrons could be suspended at various heights. Indications of a
somewhat higher standard of living than that obtaining in the
Twente *los hoes* (p. 30)) are the provision of more built-in
cupboards, the better carpentry in the cupboard beds, and the
presence of an inside privy and even two separate little rooms
partitioned off in the aisles.

Even so, the inhabitants still could not hope to live solely on
what the farm produced and where forced by dire necessity to
engage in secondary activities, producing things not for themselves or the village community but for trade further afield where

36

better markets were to be found. Many of them even went away
for a long period each year to work as wage-earners for large
concerns elsewhere in the country or abroad. The importance of
cottage industries is plainly to be seen in this farmstead, both
from the large area devoted to a weaving-room, capable of
accommodating two looms, and from the presence on the premises of a wheelwright's shop (p. 40). Other local industries apart
from weaving and the making of cartwheels included the making
of clogs, shoes and brushes, woodturning, and digging for iron
ore. In the woods oak-bark was collected for the local tanneries,
and there was also a certain amount of charcoal burning to
provide fuel for the iron foundries and other industries in the
region.

baby's chair

37

■ Parts of this aisled, timber-framed building (p. 25) may
date back to about 1750. All the outside walls originally
had wattle-and-daub panels (p. 21) but in the front wall
these were later replaced by bricks, while the other three
walls were almost completely rebuilt in brick, with mud
as mortar. The gables are clad with oak planks. The
original plan was probably that of a small *los hoes* (p. 25).
It was altered to its present form in the first half of the
nineteenth century.

gable finial

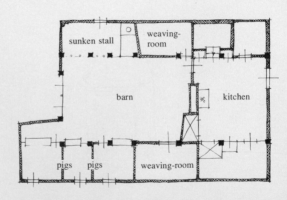

□ Although it is roughly the same shape and size as the farm from Harreveld (p. 35), this farmhouse is not a *los hoes* , as there is a partition wall between the living area and the barn. Against this wall, on the kitchen side, moreover, there is a fireplace, complete with flue and chimney to take the smoke away. Life was therefore rather more comfortable here than in a *los hoes* . Even so, it was still a very humble farm. This is obvious from a description of the area written in 1826, from which we learn that even the mud was only used as mortar in "huts and other meagre dwellings". Nor was the standard of living all that high, as can be judged from the fact that in 1838, for instance, this cottage housed two families, comprising no less than twelve people in all!

The kitchen has a floor made of little bricks. These were known as "pot waste" because they were originally a by-product of the potteries in the neighbourhood. Floors of this type, as well as floors made of pebbles laid in patterns (see No. 11), used to be common in this area and just over the border.

chair

As with the farm from Harreveld (p. 35), it was not possible to live from agriculture alone, and in the area around Beltrum (i.e. between Zutphen and Winterswijk) textiles were one of the most important cottage industries. As early as 1700 there were merchants in places like Winterwijk, Neede and Eibergen who, besides dealing in flax, were also beginning to engage in the actual process of manufacturing linen goods. They got poverty-stricken farmers in the hamlets to prepare the thread and do the weaving and then bleached the linen themselves before dispatching it to the west of the country and elsewhere. The textiles produced by the cottage weavers were on the coarse side, but much finer cloth was made in the larger villages, by specialist weavers who did not engage in farming activities. The looms they used were sometimes too big to go into their houses and had to be accommodated in a special building, a "manufactory", belonging to the manufacturer. The extent of the industry can be gauged from the fact that before 1808 in Neede alone the making of linen-damasks for table use was providing work for no less than 250 people, not counting children.

folding table

Near the farmhouse is a little bread-oven (p. 33). Bread continued to be made in many households, both in town and country, until well into the nineteenth century.

weaver's shuttle

In the barn are several farm carts from the eastern part of the country.

clothes-chest

■ As a craft, wheelmaking was one of the most developed forms of cottage industry. In this workshop wheels were made for carts and wagons, sometimes to the order of a farmer in the neighourhood, but more often for dealers in such places as Deventer, who had a wide market for all sorts of farming gear, including things like winnowing baskets, wooden shoos, seed skeps, flails (p. 26), sieves, brushes, tubs and barrels. There were numerous wheelwrights' shops in the Achterhoek, particularly around Winterswijk; records of them go back to before 1800 and in 1870 there were still several dozen in operation. They were often attached to farms, which helped to provide the basic necessities of life but were usually of secondary importance (p. 36).

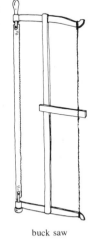

buck saw

□ The Achterhoek was a richly wooded area, with an abundance of oaks and elms, and this was doubtless one of the reasons why wheelmaking and other forms of woodworking were so highly developed there.

Though easy to describe in a few words, the process of making a wheel was one of the most difficult branches of carpentry. The hub and spokes were made from oak logs which were split and roughly hewn into shape on the large chopping-block outside. The hub was then finished off on a hand-operated lathe inside. The rim (felloe) was made up of curved segments which were cut from thick planks with a buck saw. The parts were then carefully assembled and passed on to the smith who provided an iron tyre for the rim and rings to strengthen the hub. The finished wheels were carried to the dealers by horse and cart or, later on, by train.

CLOGMAKER'S WORKSHOP

■ This workshop shows the traditional arrangement of tools and equipment used by a clogmaker, or clogger, until quite recently. The village clogmaker would make clogs to measure, taking account of his customers' requirements and the peculiarities of their feet. In the nineteenth century, however, there was also a highly developed cottage industry engaged in mass-producing clogs, albeit by hand, for people in the towns, where they were particularly popular amongst the working classes. In the village of Enter in Overijssel, for example, practically the whole working population was occupied in supplying clogs to dealers, who sent them to all parts of the country. As with other cottage industries the money earned in this way was by no means suffcient to meet the needs of the household and consequently a certain amount of farming was carried on as well, mainly by the women.

saw

☐ Clogs were mostly made from poplar or willow which, after being sawn into logs of the required length, was split into wedge-shaped billets. The billet was then shaped by axe and adze into a rough clog which was fined down on the bench with a clogger's knife. After this the clogs were firmly clamped down in pairs on another bench and hollowed out with special gouges and knives. A skilled clogger could get up to 50 pairs out of a cubic metre of wood and, by working from six in the morning to seven in the evening, could make an average of ten pairs a day. Around 1910 a village clogmaker, working in this way, would have earned ƒ 10 a week, which was fairly reasonable, but things were not nearly so favourable in the cottage industry. Anyone making clogs for a dealer could not expect to get much

billet

axe

adze

roughed-out clog

above 13 cents a pair, which meant he could scarcely earn *f* 1.50 a day, and this at a time when the weekly food bill alone (excluding meat) for a man with a wife and a child of four would have been at least *f* 5.50. "It is a wonder the inhabitants have not died out", commented a writer of the period on the village of Enter, and things were not much better elsewhere, though the price paid per pair may have been a cent or two higher. In fact it was probably only by cultivating their little patches of land, and keeping a few pigs, goats and perhaps a cow, that most people did manage to survive.

If an assistant was employed, he would get the same rate for the job as his master got from the dealer, but on the other hand it was left to him to do the heavier work of hollowing the clogs out, which took about 45 minutes per pair as against 20 minutes for the initial roughing out and 10 for the final shaping.

The workshops were generally stuffy, damp and dark as well as pokey. Many clogmakers, however, did not have a separate workshop and had to use the living-room, which was often the only room in the house. And as if all this was not bad enough, they were also up against strong competition from other people who were prepared to work for even less than they were, as is evident from the fact that between 1910 and 1915 imports of clogs from Belgium amounted to an average of 2¹/₂ million kilogrammes a year (a large pair of man's clogs weighing about one kilogramme).

Much the same sort of picture could be painted of any of the cottage handwork industries around the turn of the century. Whatever the innumerable workers employed in this way produced, whether it was shoes, nails, fastenings or cigars, they were all condemmed to lead a thoroughly miserable existence.

clogger's kunife

hollowing-out bench

SMALL VELUWE FARMHOUSE
FROM VIERHOUTEN (Gld.)

■ This little aisled building (p. 25) dates from just before 1850. The walls of the house are brick, and the barn has brick at the back and weatherboarding at the side. The entrance to the barn, which has a sunken stall (p. 26), is at the back. Nearby are two hay barracks of different types from Gelderland. These consist of one or more posts with a roof, the height of which can be adjusted according to the amount of hay stored under it.

□ Farmhouses like this, which are really miniature versions of the ones being built on the sandy soils at this period, are very common on the Veluwe. This is because in the nineteenth century there was still a lot of waste ground here, on which numerous farm labourers were able to settle and eventually, by dint of unremitting hard work, to raise themselves to the level of small independent farmers.

sheep's collar

well

Bible text

The way in which such a farm developed is graphically described in a government publication of 1908: "A labourer who had just got married and had next to nothing to his name would generally begin with a few chickens and a goat or two, the latter being kept both for their milk and for their dung, which he would spread on his little field. Gradually he would take on other animals, first a few piglets and then a calf for fattening, until eventually he would reach the stage where he was able to keep the calf and sell the milk. The waste from the dairy, together with undersized potatoes and meal from the rye he grew, would then allow him to increase his stock of pigs, which again would bring in more money, while the extra dung would enable him to bring a bit more of the heathland under cultivation. If all went well he would gradually cut down on the amount of time he went out working for other people and devote more attention to his own farm, especially if he had grown-up children who were already earning. It did not always work out so favourably, but nonetheless the small-scale farms of labourers in this area often have a salutary effect".

can for extinguishing
embers

pottery dog

GELDERLAND FARMHOUSE FROM ARNHEM (Gld.)   88

■ As well as innumerable smallholdings there were of course larger farmsteads on the Veluwe. This one is a characteristic example of a type still to be seen in considerable numbers between, say, Arnhem and Zutphen. It is the only farmhouse in the museum not to have been brought from elsewhere, having been built on the spot around 1800. Although in form it is basically the same as the farmhouse from Vierhouten (p. 43), one can clearly see, even from the outside, that more attention has been paid to living conditions. The windows are larger and there are more of them, and since there is enough space for a passageway, the front door does not have to open directly into the living-room. *The building is not open to visitors.*

wall clamp

fanlight

DAY LABOURER'S COTTAGE   12
FROM NUNSPEET (Gld.)

■ This one-roomed cottage, backed by a barn with a little
sunken stall (p. 26) for a goat and a sheep or two, is an
improved version of the type of dwelling lived in by
casual labourers. Compared with the hovels they usually
lived in, the improvements here include walls of brick and
wood instead of turves, and a floor of flagstones instead of
mud. Refinements like these were gradually introduced
towards the end of the nineteenth century and give a false
impression of the standard of living of most casual labourers in the past, especially when carefully reconstructed,
as in this case.

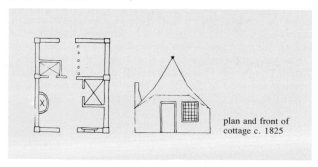

plan and front of
cottage c. 1825

tin box

milk pail

cooking-pot

☐ The cottage was originally one of a "colony" of hovels on the heathland just outside Nunspeet. The people who lived there belonged to the weakest group of workers on the land. Each spring the whole family, like many others on the Veluwe, would go off to Friesland and Drenthe, taking the goat, the sheep and the dog with them, to strip the oak trees of their bark, vast quantities of which used to be required for tanning leather. After two and a half months of hard labour, from three in the morning to nine at night, they would go home with a bit of money in their pockets to meet the baker's and grocer's bills. On this, plus casual work for farmers, a bit of poaching, and whatever other irregular work they could get (such as helping with the hay harvest), they had to get through the year as best they could.

Casual labourers formed quite a sizeable proportion of the agricultural population and were regarded as the pariahs of rural society. Outside the seasonal peaks in the demand for labour, which they naturally made the most of, they had to fend for themselves. Rather than live in sheep-pens or pigsties they often settled outside the villages and hamlets, like numerous other vagrants on the fringes of society, in hutments put up on the heath or sand drifts or in the woods. The existence of such hovels, and of whole colonies of huts in the eastern part of the country, is referred to by various writers in the early nineteenth century, and was tolerated because the farming system would have broken down without casual labour. Places where they were found included, for instance, Oldebroek (167 huts), Doorn-spijk (32), Heerde (97), Hoenderloo, near Zwolle, between Wijhe and Olst, in the Achterhoek and at Hattem. The Hattem settlement is described in a publication of 1853, from which we learn that the hovels were generally in a wretched condition, with floors below ground level, walls of turves and roofs of heather. Inside there were usually a fireplace consisting of three upright stones, and a couple of wickerwork cots, in which people slept on a sack of straw or moss laid over bundles of firewood.

Day labourers cottages in other areas were on the whole some-what better, but they had to pay rent for them out of their extremely meagre and irregular earnings, and, as there was no waste ground, there was no game, no free firewood, and no domestic animals could be kept either. Consequently the overall situation of these labourers was often even worse than that of those on the higher ground and there was certainly no question of their being able to build up little smallholdings of their own. Some nineteenth century writers compared their plight to that of, for example, the Irish, and this was by no means exaggerated, as is clear from a report drawn up in 1880 on a visit made to the Netherlands at the behest of the British government by a certain Jenkins, in which it is categorically stated that the wages, housing and food of the Dutch farm labourer were all much worse than those of his English counterpart.

DAY LABOURER'S CABIN   77
FROM ONSTWEDDE (Gr.)

■ This cabin is little more than a hole in the ground with a roof over it. Roof and walls consist mainly of turves cut from the peat, with some wooden planking on the front wall. Such places were still being built even at the beginning of this century.

□ Even the simplest of cottages (p. 48) was beyond the reach of the very poorest members of society, and in the peat-soil areas, particularly in Friesland, Groningen and Drenthe, the lowest-paid workers generally had recourse to turf cabins like this. They included peat-cutters and those who worked as casual labourers for farmers who settled on the excellent agricultularly land that was left after the peat had been removed. (It was particularly well suited to the growing of potatoes which, among other things, could be made into potato flour). When there was no other work to be had, they would fall back on making brooms or breaking stones for the roads, and if they were lucky, they might be able to supplement their meagre diet with the produce of a bit of land and a goat. On the older sandy soils of Drenthe, where the poor were generally taken care of by the community (see p. 27), there were far fewer of these hovels to be seen. It is quite wrong to suppose that this lamentable state of affairs only came into being in the nineteenth century, for there are indications that large numbers of agricultural labourers were obliged to live in more or less the same way in the seventeenth and eighteenth centuries. Such poverty-stricken people, however, generally leave little trace behind them. Written or pictorial records are very few and far between and even their dwellings are made of flimsy materials and soon fall into decay. It is not surprising therefore that the example in the museum has to be completely renewed from time to time.

49

■ Sheepcotes like this used to be common sight on the high ground extending from the eastern part of the province of Utrecht to Twente. They were sometimes situated near farmhouses, sometimes in the fields or on the heath. They would be used to house the sheep at night so that the all-important dung could be collected. In essence they were nothing more than sunken stalls (p. 26), with roofs constructed of simple trusses (p. 21) supported on posts driven into the ground, and with walls of wooden planks nailed to the inside of the posts. The whole thing was strengthened with turves and sometimes, as here, with adjustable braces as well. The fact that the wood eventually rotted away did not matter very much as it was easy enough to find new material. Consequently rough wooden constructions like this generally became a veritable patchwork in the course of time, as can be seen from the stalls in the little farmhouse from Vierhouten (p. 43).

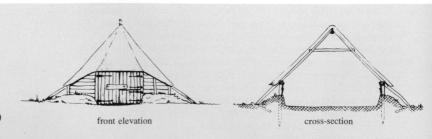

front elevation   cross-section

■ In this building, which was put in 1646, the aisled (p. 25)
barn has always been divided off from the farmhouse
proper. The latter has been altered at various times: the
parlour was built on around 1700 and fitted with cupboard
beds some time later, while the back kitchen was enlarged
to its present form around 1900. These and other modifi-
cations were, for the most part, retained when the building
was moved to the museum and in its present state it gives
an idea of a typical farm in the Betuwe area (between the
Lower Rhine and the Waal) at the end of the nineteenth
century.

headstall

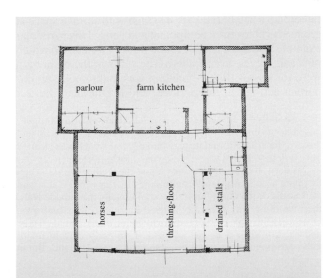

chair

51

cupboard

fly trap

In this area it was traditional for the loft above the tie-beams in the barn to be reserved for hay, which was fed in through a hatch from carts standing under cover of the specially designed overhanging roof. The grain harvest was stored in a separate barn with an adjustable roof, rather like a hay barrack (p. 43), and with storage space at ground level for farm equipment and carts. This particular example also has a lean-to round three of its sides in which pigs and calves were stalled. The stalls in the main barn were for horses (horse-breeding was traditionally an important activity in the Betuwe) and for the dairy herd.

☐ In these stalls the animals stood on a hard and sometimes slighty raised floor (instead of in a pit, as in the sunken stall, p. 26) and most of their *dung* found its way into a *gutter* which was cleaned out every day. If they stood facing the threshing-floor (p. 26), as in this barn, then the gutter ran behind the wall of the stalls and the dung was swept out through holes or flaps in the side and back walls of the barn, but if they stood facing the outside wall, then the dung was generally carried outside in wheelbarrows. Obviously this type of stall is more hygienic than the sunken type and for this reason it was adopted at an early date in major dairy-farming areas such as Friesland and North Holland. But in areas where people mainly kept cows to obtain manure, the sunken stall generally survived until the advent of artificial fertilizers in the nineteenth century.

The rich clay soils of the Betuwe were highly productive and lent themselves readily to mixed farming. Both dairy farming and meat production were long-established activities of considerable importance. Butter was made on the farms themselves (see p. 73) and on a farm of this size the milk yield was so high that a form of mechanization had to be introduced. In one of the stalls there is a large churn which was operated by a treadwheel turned by a strong dog. There was also a lot of fruit-growing and on the arable side large crops of cereal, pulses, etc. were raised, not to be used as animal feeding stuffs but to be sent to market. This diversity made for security, but on the other hand the farmers often had to contend with floods.

dog churn

Large farms on the fertile river clays in the centre and east of the country thus enjoyed a continuous prosperity which made it possible to introduce into their buildings refinements unknown in poorer areas. As early as the seventeenth century, for example, the barn and the house part were not just separated by a wall but treated as separate structural entities, with the result that the farmhouse came to be more like a town house both in construction (load-bearing walls with beams set into them) and in outward appearance. This particular farmhouse originally had brick arches above the windows (they are still visible in places) and its wall clamps proclaim its date, while the citified façade even runs to a step gable over the parlour. The T-shaped plan, which results from building the farmhouse with its axis perpendicular to that of the barn, was particularly common in the Betuwe area and along the river IJssel in Gelderland in the eighteenth and nineteenth centuries. "De Hanekamp", a farmhouse-cum-inn from Zwolle (No. 74), which dates from c. 1750, is another example.

rattle

FARMHOUSE-INN "DE HANEKAMP"   74
FROM ZWOLLE (Ov.)

■ For more than two centuries "De Hanekamp" (The Cock-pit) enjoyed an exceptional reputation in Zwolle and a wide area roundabout, not only as an inn, but also as a café and place of recreation. It was built arround 1750 and extended in 1840 with a farmhouse section built on at the back with large barn, with stalls for cows and horses. It was conveniently situated just outside the town on the main road to Salland and Twente. Many livestock dealers, after having visited the busy markets in Zwolle, unharnessed their horses there in order to settle their business and spend the night.

The inn has a taproom with an old-fashioned bar and tiled fireplace and, above the cellar vaults, a mezzanine room with cupboard beds. "De Hanekamp" is open throughout the season as a café for museum visitors.

KEMPEN FARMHOUSE FROM BUDEL (N.Br)   98

■ This long, aisled building (p. 25) comes from the Dutch
part of De Kempen, an area straddling the border with
Belgium, and some of the details of its construction sug-
gest that it may go back to 1700. All the walls are brick. In
the front wall are the door and window of the living room,
and along one of the side walls is a series of doors giving
on to, from right to left, the kitchen, the sunken stall (p.
26) for cattle, the threshing-floor (p. 26) and the sunken
stall for sheep. Originally it was quite a large farm for the
area, concentrating on arable crops such as cereals, to be
sent to market, and large quantities of green fodder for the
cattle and sheep, which supplied manure for the poor soil;
however, there was a certain amount of dairy produce as
well. Some time after 1800 it was reduced to a smallholding with only two or three cows, a draught ox and a few
sheep, and the original arrangement of living quarters and
barn was altered to a certain extent.

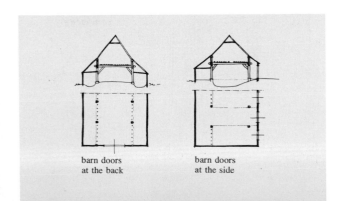

barn doors
at the back

barn doors
at the side

wall clamps

type of andiron

salt-box

☐ All the aisled barns discussed so far have been arranged in more or less the same way: a threshing-floor in the centre, underneath a loft where hay or cereals were stored; stalls in the aisles; and the main entrance in the end wall, generally facing the road. After about 1700, however, another type of arrangement became quite common, not only in Brabant but also in other areas such as Drenthe and north-east Overijssel, on farms where the need for large quantities of manure was the most important consideration. Here the sunken stalls were dug in the nave and the side walls were made higher to take doors through which carts could be driven right into the stalls, either to empty them or bring a fresh layer of turves. At the same time this meant that windows and doors for the living quarters could also be let into the higher walls, as in this particular farm where the entrance to the kitchen is in the side wall towards the road.

To make the ceiling of this kitchen the spaces between the beams have been filled in with twigs bent round to form arches and plastered with clay. In the fireplace there is a wooden crane and hanger for the pot used to boil up fodder for the animals. The cupboard beds are decorated with a rustic form of Renaissance ornament and may date from the first phase of building around 1700.

chair

lantern

hourglass

56

cross-section
of barn

passageway

plan of barn

■ The main building dates from c. 1700, with later alterations. The living quarters are built entirely of brick but the
aisled barn behind has wooden walls. The farming here
was mixed, with some cattle and some arable land. In
about 1750 the acreage was increased and a separate barn
was built to cope with the increased arable yield. A
bakehouse (p. 33) was also added. None of the buildings
is open to the public, except the barn, showing an exhibition of rural means of transport.

□ The large freestanding barn is again in the form of a nave with
two aisles (p. 25). The nave in this instance, however, served as
a "mow", where grain and hay were stacked from the floor to the
roof, and threshing (p. 26) was done in one of the aisles, which
also served as a through passageway for carts. This sort of barn,
which could vary considerably in size, was known as a "Flemish
barn" since it was common in the Belgian part of De Kempen
(cf. p. 55) as well as in adjacent parts of North Brabant. In fact
the areas on both sides of the border had a common culture, as is
very obvious when one compares this Dutch farmhouse with the
many examples, both large and small, in the Bokrijk Open-Air
Museum near Hasselt in Belgium.

FARMHOUSE FROM STAPHORST (Ov.)   22

■ This very long, aisled (p. 25) farmhouse, which has brick
walls in the living quarters and mostly wooden ones
elsewhere, was built around 1800. The adjoining villages
of Staphorst and Rouveen, strung along the old main road
from Zwolle to Meppel, are situated at the point where the
pastures on the low-lying peat soils meet the sandy soils
on the higher ground. Most of the farms concentrate on
raising cattle and for this they need an enormous amount
of hay for winter feeding. Consequently, at the back of the
barn, there is a capacious *haymow*, where hay
was stacked from floor to roof, and an entrance has been

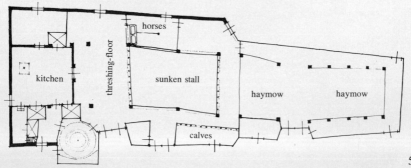

provided for the haycarts in the low side wall. The poor, sandy soil also meant, however, that a great deal of manure was needed; so there is a large sunken stall (p. 26) in the centre of the barn, with manure doors again in the side walls. The threshing-floor (p. 26) between the stall and the living quarters also served as a feedway and a small corner of it was used as a scullery.

☐ Though by no means conservative in other respects, the people of Staphorst have clung to old styles in their dress and houses longer than most other country folk and certainly much longer than townspeople. Even today their houses still retain many of the features one might have found in the past in any average farmhouse in the east of the country. For instance, the usual type of fireplace in the kitchen was, until quite recently, a direct descendant of that found in a *los hoes* (p. 25), with iron hearth plate and ash pit under a wooden hood and chimney. Other traditional items are the chest, the food cupboard, which was set beside the front door so as to form a sort of vestibule, the ladder-backed, rush-bottomed chairs, the folding table, which was propped up against the food cupboard when not in use, and the cupboard beds. Interiors like this have come to be regarded as typical of Staphorst but in fact the style only crystallized gradually from about 1850 on. Particularly characteristic are the tiles, which began to be used much more extensively on the floor and the walls at a time when they were already becoming less common in the rest of the country, and the painted woodwork and furniture, which were often further embellished with gay flowers, garlands and improving proverbs in a countrified version of the Biedermeier style that was fashionable in the early nineteenth century. This fashion was given considerable impetus by a German family of painters by the name of Goldsteen, who settled in nearby Meppel around 1825, but it also was partly due to the fact that the villagers were great traders, often journeying far from home, and were in the habit of picking up good solid secondhand cupboards and cabinets, to say nothing of richly ornamented eighteenth-century street doors and so forth, which were no longer fashionable in town.

painted ornament

chest

They never seem to have been particularly prosperous, however. Their style of life was frugal and they did not always manage to escape poverty. Around 1850, for instance, it became difficult to collect any taxes from them since their incomes were so low. Most of them were only smallholders and they were generally obliged to seek other work besides farming. They traded in cattle, horses and indeed anything they could lay their hand on; they went off as far afield as France to work as woodcutters, or Germany to do seasonal work on the land such as haymaking; they made clogs, cut peat, worked as thatchers, carriers and so on, and the deliberations of the local council were often accompanied by the clicking of knitting-needles, since people could earn money by knitting stockings and mittens. Under these conditions it was not uncommon for the whole of the farm work to fall to the lot of the woman of the household, which meant that it was left to the grandparents to bring up the children.

truck

FARMHOUSE FROM KADOELEN (Ov.)   20
IN THE VOLLENHOVE DISTRICT

■ In the course of the eighteenth century the traditional arrangement of the aisled type of farm building, in which the barn doors were in the end wall (p. 25), was gradually replaced by other forms, with specifically local variations. This example, which was probably erected around 1800 but incorporates later alterations, is typical of the form that evolved in the district of Vollenhove, where the

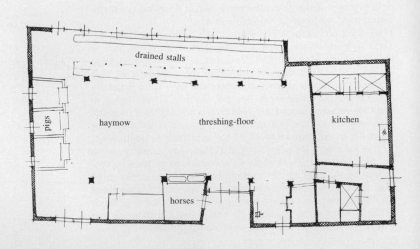

land was mainly pasture, with some arable. As in the Staphorst example (p. 59), there is a haymow at the back of the barn and the doors to this area, as well as the even larger ones to the rest ot the barn, are all built into the low side wall. The barn is separated from the living quarters by a brick wall.

knive-grinder

☐ In the mow the hay was stacked from floor to roof. Consequently there is no loft here and the bay between the posts (p. 20) could be made much wider than on the threshing-floor, over which there was a loft for storing cereals. In one of the aisles are drained stalls with manure doors (p. 52), and at the back pigsties.

There are some similarities to the Staphorst farm in the living quarters, too. In both cases, for example, the hood over the fireplace is against the front wall between the windows. The chimney here, however, is entirely of brick, and there is also a proper vestibule.

foot-warmer

churn with
plunging dasher

■ This dairy farm, built in 1832, is typical of the area of meadows and meres in north-west Overijssel. The walls of the living quarters are mainly brick, those of the barn wood, including a wooden wall between barn and house. Most of the nave of the barn, which has an extra high roof, was used as a mow (p. 59) for storing the enormous amount of hay required for winter feeding. The beams here are noticeably lighter than in barns where they had to support a loft. Between the haymow and the wall of the house was a general-purpose area used, among other things, for making butter and as a scullery.

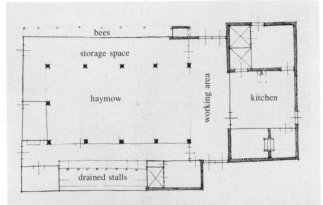

bees

storage space

haymow

working area

kitchen

drained stalls

☐ In one of the aisles of the barn is a row of simple drained stalls (p. 52) with a separate feedway (there being no arable farming and so no need for a sunken stall in which to collect manure). The other aisle served as a store for such things as peat for the fire. Peat was cut locally by the farmer himself and, apart from supplying his own needs, formed an important secondary source of income, along with fishing, reed-cutting, etc. The barn doors, which are in the side walls to allow for the haymow, are comparatively small. This was because wagons and carts were almost never used in Giethoorn, where the hay brought in from the meadows in boats and carried into the barns on handbarrows. Under the overhanging eaves at one side of the barn is a row of beehives and, as in many other old farmhouses (e.g. at Staphorst), a sand box. Fine white sand was used for scouring pots and pans, tiled floors ans steps, and every morning the flagstones inside the house were strewn with sand, sometimes, especially at weekends, in patterns.

peat-cutting spade

 eelspear

peat-scuttle

LARGE FARMHOUSE
FROM OUD-BEIJERLAND (Z.H.)

23

■ This farmhouse, which looks more like a castle, was put by a country landowner in 1617. He had it built with one more storey than usual to accommodate a series of rooms ("the lord's rooms") which he himself retained the right to use when he wanted to go hunting or stay in the

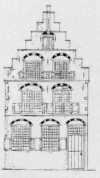

town house façade
c. 1625

farmhouse façade

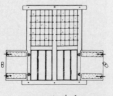

casement window

country for a while. The rest of the house was lived in by his tenant who worked the farm belonging to it on the fertile marine clays of the then newly reclaimed Hoekse Waard polders. It is built entirely of brick and in construction and style it follows contemporary town houses. The barn that originally stood behind it had long since disappeared by the time it was transferred to the museum, so a new one more or less in the style of those on the islands of South Holland has been added to give it the aspect of a farmhouse once more. The buildings are not open to the public.

☐ Land reclamation was a costly business, but the reclaimed soils in the area to the north of the Maas estuary (i.e. IJsselmonde, Hoekse Waard, Voorne and Putten, all of which were originally islands) were so fertile and produced such good surpluses that it was highly remunerative. The polder on which this farmhouse stood belonged to the famous Count Egmont, who lived in Brussels and figured so prominently in his country's history. He had it diked in 1557. The money for empoldering was usually raised by selling off part of the new land to other very wealthy financiers (who were generally also absentee landlords) and by letting the rest to tenant farmers. The soil lent itself to mixed farming on a large scale. Here livestock and arable crops could exist independently, side by side, instead of having to support one another in a cycle of fodder and manure production as they did on the sandy soils in the east of the country. Also, the variety of crops that could be produced made people less vulnerable to changes in demand. Among the important products traditionally sent to market (often an international one) were cereals, flax (for linen weaving) and madder (for paint making). One result of all this was that the type of aisled building with a large haymow in the barn and large doors in the side walls (p. 59) was already found in this area by about 1600. Some idea of a typical Beijerland farm of that period is given by the drawing in the margin, which is taken from a land surveyor's map of 1583.

farmhouse
before 1583

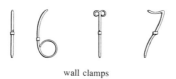

wall clamps

FARMHOUSE WITH PYRAMID ROOF FROM ZUID-SCHARWOUDE (N.H.)

■ This building dates from 1745. It is virtually square in plan, with a square haymow (p. 59) in the centre, and has a more or less pyramidal roof. The roof is supported by a framework of timbers resting on four massive wooden posts (p. 21), one at each corner of the haymow. Along

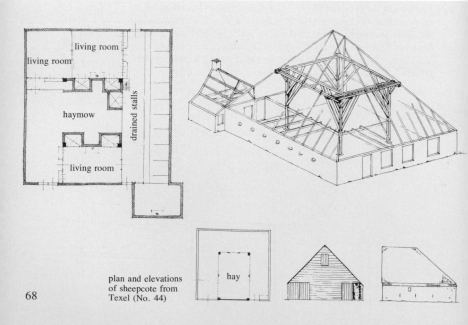

plan and elevations of sheepcote from Texel (No. 44)

one side there is a row of drained stalls (p. 52) for 18 to 20 cows, whose milk was used to make full-cream cheese. The stalls are decorated in the way they often used to be in North Holland in the summer when the cows were put out to pasture (Fig. p. 69). Besides dairy farming there will have been some arable and also some market gardening. The wood paneling and tiled fireplaces in the living quarters are in a style often found in North Holland in the eighteenth century, not only in farmhouses but also in the houses of well-to-do people such as merchants and manufacturers in the Zaan area, Waterland and elsewhere.

bucket

☐ This is another example of a structure adapted to accommodate the huge haymow that was needed to store hay for winter feeding. In this respect it may be compared with the barn at the back of the farm from Giethoorn (p. 64). There, however, the solution was to modify the traditional structure of the building, whereas here a completely new solution has been found. The

cheese-mould

result, as is obvious from the ground plan, is a thoroughly functional design, specifically suited to the needs of this type of farm, and as such it represents one of the last phases in an age-old development involving the positioning of cattle and hay. Thus the distance between the two has been minimized (especially as there are feeding hatches above the stalls) and, what is more, the heat given off by the haymow in winter has been used to good advantage by arranging the cupboard beds in brick niches round the sides. This was not the only solution, however. Other variants were developed in Friesland (p. 71), Wieringen and the Frisian Islands, and in this connection it is interesting to note that the sheepcote from Texel (No. 44) is really nothing more than a pyramidal structure cut through the middle, with stalls arranged around a central haymow.

To make the cheese unskimmed milk was warmed over the fire and rennet was added to make it curdle. When the curds had formed, a curd knife was drawn through them to break them up so that the whey would come to the top and could be ladled off. The curds were then put into moulds and left in the cheese press (Fig. p. 69) to squeeze out further moisture. After an hour or two the moulds were removed from the press, salt was added and the cheeses were put on a rack in the stalls to dry. The final products were the famous Edam cheeses.

There were numerous regional markets for dairy produce (the one at Alkmaar is still a tourist attraction) and as early as the seventeenth century great quantities of cheese and butter were being exported to England, France, Spain, Portugal, Italy and the Southern Netherlands, by way of staples like Amsterdam and Rotterdam.

curd knife

foundation stone

groat cupboard

FRISIAN FARMSTEAD FROM MIDLUM (Fr.)   78

■ This is a mixed arable and dairy farm from the fertile marine clays in the part of Friesland known as the Bouwhoek, to the north-east of Harlingen. The layout is an example of what is often called a "head, neck and body" type of farmstead. The "head" is a neat little farmhouse built in exactly the same way as contemporary houses in towns and villages, with a tiled roof and load-bearing brick walls. It contains the parlour, etc. and behind it, in the "neck" and "shoulder" of the barn, are the kitchen, churn room and milk cellar. The barn is an enormous aisled structure (p. 25) which was rebuilt in 1778 (the plans for this operation being still extant). In the nave are large mows (p. 59) for hay and cereal crops, with a

coffee mill

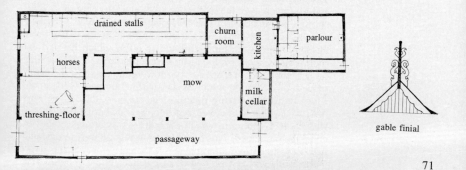

gable finial

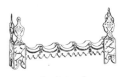

bucket rack

muckbarrow

rocking-horse

threshing-floor (p. 26) at the back complete with horse-driven threshing-machine. The aisle leading off the churn room houses a row of drained stalls (p. 52), while the other one, with a large door at either end, serves as a passageway.

☐ The long barn, with large mows in the centre under a high roof and a pasageway at the side to facilitate stacking (Fig. p. 118) is strongly reminiscent of the "Flemish" barns of North Brabant and Belgium (p. 58). It is quite different in form from the farmbuilding from North Holland (p. 68), which has living-rooms, stalls, etc., grouped round a central square haymow, but research has shown that both types were the result of the same process of evolution which began with a comparatively small structure housing living quarters and stalls, with separate hay barracks (which later developed into separate barns), and ended with a vast building in which everything was brought together under the same roof. This type of farm was common in Friesland in the seventeenth century and was technically very advanced for that period, with a high degree of mechanization: compare the

threshing-machine here with the flail on p. 26, and the churning
mechanism, driven by the horse-mill in the barn (visble through
the hatch in the churn room), with the hand churn on p. 32.
Butter making, in fact, was an extremely important activity in
this area. The first step in the process was to leave the milk in the
milk cellar in flat, oval copper pans (creamers) until the cream
had come to the top and could be skimmed off. The cream was
then put into a churn and agitated vigorously with a dasher (a
longhandled plunger with holes in it) until it coalesced to form
butter. The butter was salted to preserve it and eventually passed
into the hands of middlemen to be sold, some of it being
exported via Harlingen to countries such as England.
One of the notable things about Dutch agriculture is the contrast
between the farms on the older, poorer soils in the east to the
country, North Brabant and elsewhere, which were generally
small and belonged to the people who worked them, and those
on the fertile reclaimed land, which were frequently larger but
run by tenants. Thus most of the large farms in Friesland,
including this one, belonged to absentee landlords who lived in
places like Weesp, Amsterdam, Zeist and Utrecht; and they
were well worth having, as their high yields meant one could
charge a correspondingly high rent.

creamer

churn

ornamental bowl

73

OLDAMBTSTER FARMHOUSE 80
FROM BEERTA (Gr.)

■ This farmhouse is an example of what is known as the Oldambtster type, which in the first half of the 18th century began to spread over the south of Groningen (in Westerwolde and the Oldambt, on the denuded land of the peat colonies and further west as far as the Westerkwartier) and the north of Drenthe. On account of the ravages of cattle plague at that time these farms were from the start used mainly for arable purposes. The barns were closely similar to those of Friesland in construction and arrangement (*cf.* the drawing on p. 71).

This farmhouse, "Kloostergare" (Cloister Garth), which in its original form dates from 1796, exhibits the transitional stage between the early way of farming, as represented by, for example, the Frisian farm, and more modern methods. This transition, which took place at the beginning of the present century, may be seen in, among other things, the way the buildings have been adapted (*e.g.* the sloping wall with large doors, calculated to suit the turning-circle of larger mechanized farm machinery) and from changes in the arrangement and installation (in the living-quarters, for instance).

□ The similarity between this barn and those of the Frisian farmhouses is no accident, for in fact the barn developed in Friesland was simply taken over in the Oldambster farmhouse and combined with the house part of the older farmhouse with stalls for animals (see p. 72). The transition between the two parts is marked by indentations in the side walls. Above the house was added a loft for the storage of threshed grain, which could be reached from the barn.

Originally the house was actually lived in and it was not until a later period that there came to be living-quarters – and for the hands sleeping-quarters as well – in the barn, while a room at the front was set aside as a showpiece.

The farmhouse is, for the rest, fairly soberly appointed, but despite this there certainly existed a measure of prosperity, at any rate for the farmer. The holdings of land gradually became quite large, up to 50 hectares or so, on which were grown wheat, rye, oats and caraway and, from the middle of last century, potatoes for use in distilling and flour-making. Threshing was done in the open part of the barn. In this example the hollowed-out stones in which the pivot for the threshing-machine was placed are still in the floor. In order to allow enough room for the machine to turn round, the heavy supporting posts were placed at an angle at that point.

The farm girls and labourers originally lived with the farmer and his family, but later, as we have seen, they were banished to the back premises, where they had little privacy – witness, among other things, the two-seater privy with no doors at the back by the horse's stall.

For the rest, the farmer did not own the land but had tenancy rights over it, which dated from the Reformation, when the monastic lands were confiscated by the city of Groningen. Originally there was a tenancy agreement whereby a quit-rent had to be paid by the one side and (should the agreement be ended) compensation by the other for the farmhouse built on the land. In the 18th and 19th centuries this regulation was changed in such a way that the rent (now a lump sum) became non-with-drawable and "everlasting" and the land might be bequeathed or transferred to others by the tenant, now a perpetual leaseholder. As a result of this the farmer was in practice virtually able to dispose of the land as if he were the owner.

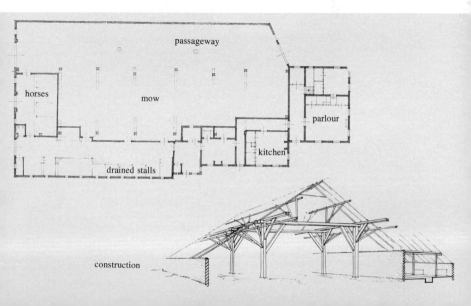

passageway

horses

mow

parlour

kitchen

drained stalls

construction

MERCHANT'S HOUSE
FROM KOOG ON THE ZAAN (N.H.) 34

■ Behind the façades, which are partly of brick, is a house
built virtually entirely of wood, which consists of several
wings. The oldest part of it, dating from 1686, is not open
to the public. In 1740 this was extended by a wing along
the street and around 1770 a third wing was built on at
rights-angles to the street and the whole building was
modernized in accordance with contemporary taste,
acquiring outside walls partly of brick and wooden gables
with crests and other carving. Later on the street doors
were replaced by the present ones. Thus this merchant's
house grew into a building of a U-shaped plan round a
central courtyard – the "back yard" as it was called –
which in its original situation, as on its present site in the
museum, looked out over water, i.e. over the river Zaan, a
waterway of the greatest importance to the old industrial
area of North Holland.

□ The interior is mainly installed in accordance with the taste of the
well-to-do bourgeoisie towards the end of the 19th century. This
naturally tells most strongly in the drawing-room. Older pieces
of furniture, which did not fit in with the new modes, were
removed from there to less important rooms. So is was that the

clock

77

beautifully painted "Assendelft" sideboard, dating from about 1700, was banished to the counting-house.

The first room on the right as one goes through the door of the house, was the counting-house. There the merchant did his extensive book-keeping. The Zaan merchants had fingers in numerous pies, including the timber trade and sawmilling, ship-building, oil-milling and the oil trade, papermaking, whaling, sailmaking, paint manufacture, the fur trade and baking (ship's biscuits). Behind the counting-house is a kitchen, with a typical North-Holland chimney-piece faced with the tiles painted with Biblical subjects, which were produced in large quantities at that period. Next to this is a partitioned-off section with a cupboard bed. Here one can clearly see the way the house is constructed, with load-bearing posts, beams and panelling all in wood and only the fireplace and chimney flue in brick.

fireplace

At the back of this wing is a sun parlour. Every merchant's house had a room like this, preferably overlooking the Zaan. It is a sort of conservatory with numerous windows, where people could take coffee or tea in moments of leisure. Here the men smoked their long clay pipes and enjoyed a drink and the women sat over their fancy-work. Sometimes the master of the house would also keep his collection of scientific apparatus here, such as machines for producing electricity, etc. Round games were also played here, but what people particularly enjoyed was watching the busy traffic of the boats on the river Zaan.

wall tile

In the front room – the salon or "best end" as it was called in old Zaan parlance – we find furniture and decoration of the end of the last century. Black polished furniture, red plush upholstery and portraits in oval black frames were highly characteristic of that period.

Opposite the house is the garden or pleasance, with a parterre of "embroidery": clipped hedges and patterns in grass and in the centre a sundial surrounded by beds with glass beads laid out in designs. These beads were mainly made in glass factories in Amsterdam in the 17th and 18th centuries to the commission of the Dutch East and West India Companies, who used them for trading in the tropics. At home a use was found for them in laying out small gardens in place of tropical shells, which were also very expensive at that time.

chair

The designs in which the beads are laid out feature the arms of Smit and Honig, those of the couple who lived in the merchant's house in the first half of the 19th century, along with those of their mothers, De Jager and Appel, and some flower motifs. Round about lie beds of flowers and vegetables. Normally such gardens were much larger, up to 3000–7000 square metres, but there did also exist small ones like this, which is only 225 square metres. Obviously lacking here are the hotbeds and cold frames, the orchard and the park. To protect the plants from the wind a garden like this would be surrounded by a fence, which here makes a fine background with a summer-house.

COACH-HOUSE WITH HOUSE AT THE BACK-
FROM THE ZAAN AREA (N.H.)   40

■ This wooden building is an example of a coach-house of
the first quarter of the 19th century. In it is housed the
merchant's carriage and here too were stored in summer
the sleigh and ice boat, the status symbols of the rich
merchants of those days.

□ The house at the back, a lean-to with a roof sloping one way, is
the smallest possible type of dwelling: a single room with a
cupboard and a cupboard bed, a tiny porch that also served as a
kitchen and a minute attic. This was how working-people lived.
For a house like this they still have had to pay a rent of around
ƒ 1.50 a week at the beginning of this century and that out of
wages that mostly did not go above 5 guilders a week. Yet the
inhabitants of such a place – mostly older couples with married
children – somehow managed to save a bit nonetheless!

Hindeloopen
façade c. 1700

rotatable trivet

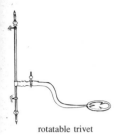

kettle

■ This building is not original but the façade gives some idea of the type of façade often found in the little Zuyder Zee port of Hindeloopen in the days when it boasted a considerable population of well-to-do master mariners and other seafaring men. Inside, an attempt has been made, using materials such as tiles, painted furniture and woodwork that are largely authentic, to show what the "best room" in such a house would have looked like shortly before 1800.

□ The mariners of Hindeloopen owed their prosperity in the seventeenth and eighteenth centuries to the trade they did with Scandinavia and the Baltic countries, carrying goods for the entrepreneurs of Amsterdam and Zaandam. On their frequent visits to Amsterdam they were able to buy fine things made there as well as imported luxuries such as porcelain from China and Japan and chintzes from India, to say nothing of picking up the latest fashions in furniture and interior decoration generally. Thus they shared the taste for richly carved oak furniture that developed during the seventeenth century amongst the wealthier inhabitants of Holland and Friesland (cf. the fine cupboard in this room) and also in the fashion for painted furniture which became popular in the towns around the Zuyder Zee towards the end of the century. The cupboard beds here show how people liked to have large wooden surfaces embellished with pictures copied from Bible illustrations or scenes of everyday life, the theme in this case being various aspects of rope-making, a trade of the utmost importance to seafarers. Few pieces of furniture escaped elaborate decoration at this time except, curiously enough, chairs which in Hindeloopen were generally painted in plain colours only.

If, however, the people of Hindeloopen were merely participating in the general taste of various periods, how was it that rooms like this, which one might have seen in any number of places in the past, came to be regarded as typical Hindeloopen interiors? The answer would seem to be that due to a marked decline in Amsterdam's trade around 1800, Hindeloopen shrank from a prosperous adjunct of the capital to an isolated fishing village which at the same time had little in common with the farming community throughout the rest of Friesland. As a result the style of its houses crystallized, so that when the first tourists appeared on the scene around 1880, it was almost inevitable that they should think of it as something unique to Hindeloopen. In the event this enabled the Hindeloopers to develop a considerable industry in painted furniture which was primarily produced for outsiders.

folding table

cap-box

FISHERMAN'S COTTAGE 43
FROM MARKEN (N.H.)

■ This cottage, like all the cottages on the island of Marken in the Zuyder Zee (now the IJsselmeer), is entirely of wood. It probably dates from c. 1750 and was built on an artificial mound as a safeguard against the floods which were a constant menace before the advent of the enclosing dike. Immediately inside the front door there is a butt in which rainwater from the roof was collected for use as drinking water. There are only two rooms, a small "best room" and a large living room, which has a wooden partition, or speer, by the front door to prevent the draught reaching the fireplace. Instead of a chimmey to take the smoke away there is a wooden shutter in the roof, which can be opened and closed from below by means of a rope. The most striking feature of the interior is the superabundance of ornaments which are heaped or hung up in every available space.

They include plates, which generally have a hole bored in them so that they can be suspended by means of a cord made fast with a wooden toggle or a knot, and numerous pictures of members of the House of Orange (the inhabitants of Marken being nothing if not royalists).

pot hanger

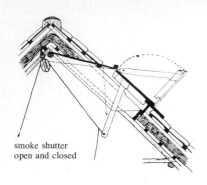

smoke shutter
open and closed

chip box

method of hanging
a plate, back
and front

clog

☐ The cupboard beds were not only places to sleep in but played an important part in the decoration of the interior, being made up for show in the daytime, in accordance with a custom that was not exclusive to Marken but was common all over the north-eastern part of the country. Painted furniture and other objects, which were as popular in Marken as they were in Hindeloopen, were generally imported from elsewhere. Oval chip boxes, for instance, came from Germany, A notably seamanlike feature of this interior is the adjustable pot hanger made of cord threaded through a block of wood with two holes in it.

For all their charm these cottages had their drawbacks. The absence of a chimney and of any sanitary arrangements can scarcely have been beneficial to health. At all events they have been blamed for the high death-rate from tuberculosis among the island's population and for their poor resistance to disease.

In the late middle ages, when the island was larger than it is now and formed part of the mainland, cattle farming was the main means of subsistance but later on, probably as a result of the erosion of the boggy soil in storms and gales, it became virtually impossible to keep this up on a viable scale and people turned to the sea for their livelihood. In the seventeenth and eighteenth centuries they engaged in whaling in Scandinavian waters and herring fishing round the Dogger Bank. This brought them a certain prosperity which found expression in the "best rooms", the treasures of which included souvenirs brought back from Scandinavia, Scotland and England. In the nineteenth century whaling declined in importance and competition from other fishing-villages made the herring fishery less lucrative and so they took to fishing nearer home in the Zuyder Zee, exchanging their North Sea boats for craft more suited to shallower waters.

ship in a bottle

85

■ They had their boats built elsewhere but they maintained them on the island itself, in the boatyard known as "De Hoop" which has now come to the museum. Here there is a wooden capstan for hauling the boats up out of the water and a workshop which is built of wood like the cottages and has a raised floor to escape flooding. In the workshop is a collection of shipwright's fools.

TOLL COLLECTOR'S HOUSE 113
FROM ZUIDLAREN (Dr.)

coffee urn

88

■ This brick tollhouse, with its wooden tollgate, was built about 1850 on a paved road (*steenweg*) in Zuidlaren, near the border between the provinces of Groningen and Drenthe. It has a small barn with stalls at the back and is similar in style to No. 57, from the village of Bedum in Groningen. Large numbers of these houses were built for working and lower middle class families in the area round the town of Groningen, and many more were put up along the canals in the "peat colonies", where people were settled in the nineteenth century to exploit the land left after the removal of the peat. In some cases the house was slightly larger than either of the examples in the museum and had a smallholding attached.

shot-gun

TOLTARIEF

op den STEENWEG tusschen den grooten weg der eerste klasse No. 1 bezuiden de gemeente HAREN en de gemeente ZUIDLAREN.

Bij de aankomst aan een der tolboomen zal voor tol moeten worden betaald:

Voor rij- of voertuigen met *vier* wielen voor elk aangespannen paard, ezel, muilezel of runderbeest f 0.15

Voor rij- of voertuigen met *twee* wielen, mitsgaders sleden, voor elk aangespannen paard, ezel, muilezel of runderbeest . . . . - 0.10

Drie wielen aan een rijtuig worden gerekend voor *vier.*

Voor elk gezadeld paard of muilezel . . . . - 0.07 1|2

Voor elk paard, gespannen voor eene hessenkar met *twee* of *vierwielen* . . . . - 0.30

Voor diligences of postwagens, ingerigt voor niet meer dan *zes* personen, voor elk paard . . - 0.15

Voor meer dan *zes*, doch niet meer dan *negen* personen . . . . - 0.17 1|2

Idem, voor meer dan *negen* personen . . . . - 0.20

Voor elken bok, geit of hond, gespannen voor rij- of voertuig met *twee* wielen . . . - 0.01 1|2

Idem voor rij- of voertuig met *vier* wielen . . . . - 0.03

Voor de tolbetaling wegens bovengemelde voorwerpen zal een bewijs worden verstrekt, tegen afgifte waarvan men aan den *tweeden* tolboom van de betaling zal zijn vrijgesteld.

Wegens na te melden voorwerpen zal de tol aan ieder tolhek worden geheven zonder afgifte van bewijs en zal worden betaald:

Wegens elk los paard of muilezel . . . . - 0.03

     „   „   „ runderbeest of ezel . . . . - 0.01 1|2

     „   „   „ schaap, kalf of varken . . . . - 0.01

Wanneer een kudde schapen of varkens sterker is dan *vijftig* stuks in eens . . . . - 0.50

Wegens een bespannen boerenwagen, onverschillig waarmede geladen of geheel ongeladen, en hetzij naar Groningen gaande of vandaar terugkomende op de gewone weekmarktdagen der stad Groningen - 0.02 1|2

Wegens bespannen boerenwagens in de gevallen als boven op den nademiddag en avond voor die weekmarktdagen naar Groningen gaande . . . . - 0.05

Hiervan zijn echter uitdrukkelijk uitgezonderd zoodanige boerenwagens of korrewagers, waarvan, uithoo'de hunne zitbanken op veren, riemen of andere rekbare ligchamen zijn geplaatst, de personele belasting op de paarden in hoogere klassen dan van landbouwers is verschuldigd of zoodanige boerenwagens, welke door gepatenteerde voerlieden gebezigd worden tot vervoer tegen vrachtloon van personen of goederen, welke alle aan het algemeen tarief van tol blijven onderworpen.

De bovenstaande bepalingen betrekkelijk den markttol zijn van geene toepassing op den Zuidlaarder herfstmarktdag, wanneer die gelijk tot dusverre invalt op een Groninger weekmarktdag, en zal op dien dag de tol naar het gewoon tarief zonder onderscheid worden geheven. Desgelijks zullen tusschen beide de gabellen wonende particulieren evenzeer als ingezetenen van het gehucht GLIMMEN niet meer dan den halven tol verschuldigd zijn.

Indien een gedeelte van den Nederlandschen cent zal verschuldigd zijn, zal steeds een halve cent worden gevorderd.

Wanneer bij het ontstaan van dooi weder na ingevallen vorst de passage op den grooten Rijksweg bij verordening van het Provinciaal of andere Besturen voor vrachtwagens mogt zijn gestremd, zullen zoodanige vrachtwagens gedurenden zoodanigen tijd op den onderwerpelijken weg NIET worden toegelaten, dan tegen betaling van den VIERDUBBELEN tol.

☐ The fairly large, dark red bricks used here are characteristic of the area, but the roof, with its decorative tiling, overhanging eaves and monumental chimney is rather distinctive and serves to emphasize the vaguely official nature of the building. The thousands of toll houses that used to bar the roads not only made many goods more expensive for the consumer but also caused considerable delays, which was why the keeper often ran an inn or tavern as well. The right to levy tolls was usually granted by licence.

clock

cupboard

BREWERY AND BAKEHOUSE
FROM ULVENHOUT (N.Br.)

99

■ This building from Ulvenhout, together with its contents, most of which are from Sint-Oedenrode, gives some idea of a small village brewery as it might have looked in the nineteenth century. Like most country breweries in Brabant, it was attached to an inn ("De Roskam", now demolished), and usually the proprietor of such an establishment was one of the more prosperous inhabitants of the village, supplying beer not only for his own tavern but also for others nearby which did not have a brewery themselves but which may have had a small farm attached instead. There is a bakehouse built on at the side.

hop

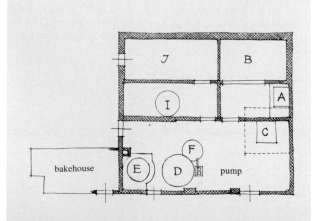

☐ Beer used to be the normal drink for most people, and Dutch beer, especially from the west of the country, was renowned both at home and abroad. The reputation of breweries like those in Haarlem, Gouda and Delft, for example, was already well established as far back as the fifteenth century, and the duty raised on the beer they sold was an important economic factor. Apart from the "merchant" breweries, however, there were also the "home" breweries, which produced beer for their own use and for others in the neighbourhood. Mostly run by women, they were to be found almost everywhere, in towns and villages as well as scattered about the countryside; so it is not surprising that they should have fallen foul of the larger concerns from time to time, until eventually there activities were restricted by law. But then gradually, from about 1600 on, the restrictions were relaxed again, and in the eighteenth and nineteenth centuries every little town, village and hamlet in Brabant and Limburg had its own brewery, with its own special brew.

grain shovel

The process of brewing is based on a chemical reaction in which starch is converted into sugar and thence into alcohol. The material normally used to provide the starch was barley. This was first softened by being steeped in a bath of water (A) and then spread out on a floor (B) where it was kept moist and continually turned in order to promote germination and prevent the development of mildew. During germination some of the starch in the barley was converted into soluble sugars, but this was subsequently stopped by drying on a metal rack in a oast-kiln (C). The dry, germinated grain (malt) was ground or crushed, dressed (i.e. purified), and then transferred to a tun (D) where it was mashed. This was done by adding hot water from a large copper heated over a brick oven (E) and stirring thoroughly so that the sugars dissolved. The resulting pulp (the mash) was drawn off into a tub (F) (leaving behing a sediment to be used as cattle feed) and from here it was pumped up into tanks in the loft, where vents in the roof ensured rapid cooling.

paddle for stirring

After cooling, the mash was run down into the copper (E), where it was boiled to give what was known as the wort, and perhaps hops would be mixed in to give it a bitter taste. The wort was then taken via the sump (F), pump and cooling tanks again, to the fermenting vat (I), where the sugars were fermented with yeast, to give alcohol and carbon dioxide. However, before the fermentation had actually stopped the liquor from the vat was drawn off into barrels and the process was allowed to continue while these were stored in the cellar (J) waiting to be delivered. Thus the finished beer was the result of hours of effort requiring both skill and judgment, and it was this of course which ultimately determined its flavour and quality.

beer barrel

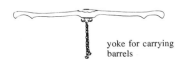

yoke for carrying barrels

HORSE-DRIVEN OIL MILL
FROM ZIEUWENT (Gld.)

1

nose bag

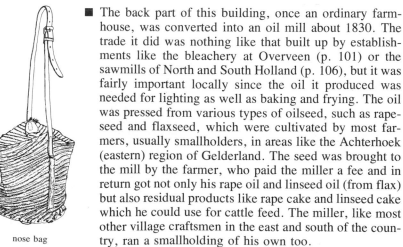

■ The back part of this building, once an ordinary farm-house, was converted into an oil mill about 1830. The trade it did was nothing like that built up by establish-ments like the bleachery at Overveen (p. 101) or the sawmills of North and South Holland (p. 106), but it was fairly important locally since the oil it produced was needed for lighting as well as baking and frying. The oil was pressed from various types of oilseed, such as rape-seed and flaxseed, which were cultivated by most far-mers, usually smallholders, in areas like the Achterhoek (eastern) region of Gelderland. The seed was brought to the mill by the farmer, who paid the miller a fee and in return got not only his rape oil and linseed oil (from flax) but also residual products like rape cake and linseed cake which he could use for cattle feed. The miller, like most other village craftsmen in the east and south of the coun-try, ran a smallholding of his own too.

The power to drive mills like this was provided by a horse (or sometimes an ox) which because it had to keep going round in circles had to be blinkered, and because of the enormous strain involved had to be changed every two hours. The horse was harnessed to a pole connected to the shaft of the crusher, which consisted of two heavy stone wheels designed to crush the seeds to a pulp. From here the pulp was transferred to a stove, where it was heated with constant stirring in order to increase the yield of oil during the actual pressing. The stirring mechanism was driven from the heavy horizontal shaft mounted above the beams, which in turn was geared to the shaft of the crusher. The heated pulp was then poured into woollen bags with leather facings and the bags were placed in the huge wooden press, where they were repeatedly stamped by a wedge hammered home by a machine rather like a double piledrive. Essentially this comprised two heavy upright balks (the stamps), each of which was raised in turn by the gearing at the end of the horizontal shaft and then allowed to fall again under its own weight. One of the stamps hammered the wedge responsible for the pressing, while the other struck an inverted wedge in order to knock the first one free again. All in all, it was a noisy business which could be heard all over the neighbourhood. The oil thus produced was collected in pans placed under the press, the average output for a ten- to twelve-hour day being about forty litres.

In many areas oil presses were also installed in wind-mills and water-mills, in which the machinery may have been a little more complicated but the principle was the same. In country districts these mills were generally local businesses with a strong tradition of craftsmanship, and some may even have been run in conjunction with a corn mill. In the more industrialized coastal area in the west of the country, however, where there were numerous oil mills scattered amongst all the other industrial mills, they were much larger and more sophisticated and the craft tradition was entirely lacking. There is one still in operation, and open to visitors, in the *Zaanse Schans,* near Zaandijk.

leather-faced
press bag

pitcher

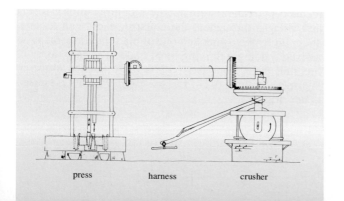

press   harness   crusher

HORSE MILL FOR GROATS
FROM WORMERVEER (N.H.)

stone-dressing
reminder board

■ In the Low Countries groats, i.e. the hulled and coarse-ground grains of cereals, were mainly prepared from buckwheat. They were a very cheap and hence staple food, especially before the widespread acceptance of the potato. Mostly they were used for making gruel and porridge, and people still use them nowadays to make a semolina-type pudding. Up to the beginning of the nineteenth century there were hundreds of groat mills in towns and villages throughout the country, each with its own shop run by the owner and one of his sons, or perhaps an assistant, doing a thriving local trade. The machinery in this mill dates from about 1770 and remained in use at Wormerveer until 1921. The builing in which it is housed is not original.

☐ As will be seen from the accompanying diagram, all the machinery was actuated by means of wooden pinions, belts and pulleys running off a large wooden cogwheel (T) pivoted on an upright wooden shaft (S), which was turned by one or, when operating to capacity, two horses (P).

First, however, the buckwheat, which the miller bought from the corn chandler, was roasted on a perforated iron tray (E) over a brick kiln (O). It was then transferred to a multiple sieve, or sifter (BZ), and from there fed to a groat crusher (A) containing a pair of furrowed stones, the upper one of which (the runner) was rotated so that the grains were crushed and roughly broken. The resulting grits, as they were termed, passed to another sifter, called a jumper (BRZ), were they were graded into different sizes (qualities), and finally the various grades were purified of any remaining husks and dust in one of the three groat machines (W).

A groat machine consists of a simple casing with a fan inside to blow out lighter particles and is similar to the winnowing machines used on farms to separate the chaff from the grain after threshing. The farm machine, however, usually had to be worked by hand and by no means every farmer had one. Those without had to resort to the use of winnowing baskets with which they tossed the threshed grain in the wind so that the light chaff

runner

mill bill

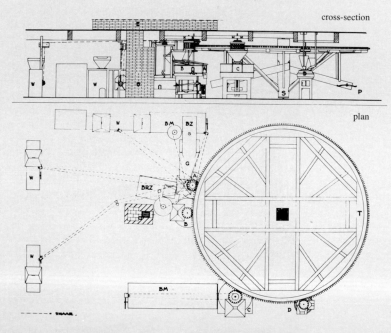

cross-section

plan

95

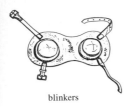

blinkers

was carried away and only the heavy kernels were left behind. Besides groats, the mill also supplied buckwheat flour (for pancakes, etc.), cattle feed and mustard. The flour was done with another pair of stones (C) similar to the first but with different furrowing, so that the grain was ground rather merely crushed. It was then dressed (separated from the meal in two bolters (BM) containing sieves of fine cloth stretched on rotatable reels. The grain for cattle feed was broken with a third pair of stones (B), while the mustard seed was pulverized with a fourth (D).

All the stones had to be dressed (sharpened) regularly, with the aid of a mill bill, and there is even a board to remind the miller when the next "servicing" was needed.

G.van Dillewijn
GRUTTER
WORMERVEER.

nameplate

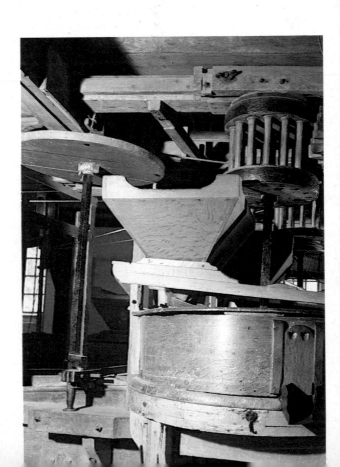

POST MILL FROM HUIZEN (N.H.)   55

■ In a post mill all the machinery is housed in an upright
wooden body (the buck) which stands and pivots on a
hefty wooden post (whence the name). Some of the thrust
of the wind, however, is also taken by the tail which
consists of steps and a pole (tail pole) for turning the
whole mill round. This particular example, which is
smaller than most, was used to grind corn. A hoist for
raising sacks of corn and meal can be seen under the small
hood above the gallery at the back. This was driven from
the shaft connected to the sails. The millstones in the buck
itself are encased in a wooden tun (see pp. 95 and 98) into
which the grain was fed from a hopper with a tapered shoe
and from which the meal ran down through a trough or
spout into sacks. Many parts of this mill are two to three
hundred years old.

☐ Post mills were common all over the Low Countries as far back as the middle ages. They are often depicted in medieval miniatures and are an interesting example of the way medieval builders thought in wood, which they used for everything, including the roof and moving parts like shafts and cogwheels. It is also typical that the only method they had of getting the sails to face square into the wind was to turn the whole buck on its post. This process was called winding and was done by using the winch on the tail to wind-in a rope or chain that had been hitched to one of a series of low posts set in a circle round the mill.

At a period when wind and water were the only other sources of energy apart from men and animals, no-one was allowed to build or operate a mill without first having purchased the franchise to use this energy from the lord of the manor or other relevant authority. The landowner, however, could build a mill himself, in which case he would usually lease it to a miller, and he also possessed what were known as "soke rights", whereby he could compel all those living in the area to have their corn ground at his mill and no-one else's. Manorial franchises like this were eventually abolished by Napoleon about 1800, but the old system of paying the miller with scoops of corn he had ground, which he could then sell, did not die out altogether for another hundred years.

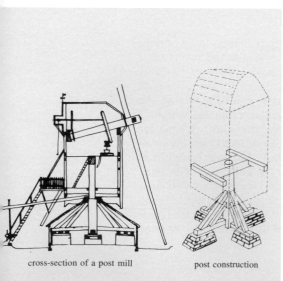

cross-section of a post mill   post construction

millstones

TOWER MILL FROM DELFT (Z.H.)   90

■ This mill, which is about 26 metres high, is in the form of a brick tower with a wooden stage round it and a thatched cap to carry the sails. The stage was used for setting the sail and also for winding. As with the post mill (p. 97), winding was done by means of a winch on the end of the tail, but in this case the tail is a triangular set of braces reaching down to the stage and only the cap and sails were turned. Inside the building, which underwent repeated alterations between 1700 and 1900, there are several floors with four sets of millstones (p. 98) and other equipment rather similar to that in the horse mill described on p. 94.

□ The principle of the rotating cap was invented towards the end of the sixteenth century and from then on brick tower mills steadily ousted the cramped and limited post mills, especially in the west of the country. To catch sufficient wind, particularly in the towns, higher and higher towers had to be built, with the result that there was often not only room for the miller to live on the premises but more space to build extra floors for the accommodation of all kinds of wind-powered machinery. The development was also helped along by the growing sophistication in the use of gears, and as a consequence the tower mill came to be the type most commonly employed for industrial purposes in the towns. In fact tower mills used to be quite a feature of places like Rotterdam, Schiedam and Delft, many of them in the service of breweries.

LAURY FROM OVERVEEN
NEAR HAARLEM (N.H.)   56

■ These brick buildings were originally laid out, perhaps
before 1700, as a bleachery. After various alterations,
however, particularly after 1800, it was eventually converted onto a laundry, where better-off families from
Amsterdam and thereabouts used to send their linen to be
done once or twice a year. The equipment includes a
boiler with hot water tank, a copper (for boiling the wash),
large tubs sunk into the floor (for soaking and rinsing) and
an impressive horse-mill-type system for pounding the
linen in the baths of warm suds. The pounders worked off
the huge camshaft which runs above the beams to the
gearing connected to the actual horse-driven shaft. They
were essentially a mechanized form of the tub and dolly

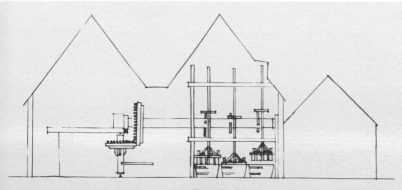

pounder mechanism

"which grandmother used" and a forerunner of the first wooden washing machines. After being washed, the linen was bleached and then finished off in a mangle. In the nineteenth century bleaching was still done by spreading the washing out in the sun on what was known as the bleaching ground. The mangles in this laundry consist of wooden rollers pressed down and rotated by a heavily weighted wooden casing which is wound back and forth. The buildings are in three parallel and adjoining sections, part of which (not open to the public) used to be lived in by the owner of the bleachery. The small bay built on at the front served as a lookout to guard against any thieving from the bleaching ground.

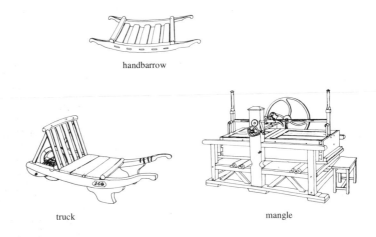

handbarrow

truck

mangle

laundry in its original surroundings, 1864

☐ Though in our eyes these buildings may seem rather domestic and picturesque, they are in fact an important industrial monument: a reminder of the famous linen bleacheries of Kennemerland that commanded such a high reputation throughout Europe in the sixteenth and seventeenth centuries. Kennemerland is a sand-dune area to the north of Haarlem and the excellence of its bleacheries was due to the purity of the water from the dunes. Their existence was one of the reasons why linen weaving in Haarlem began to develop into an important export industry from about 1500 on. This trade was boosted even further by the influx of Flemish weavers, bleachers and textile merchants after 1580, as well as by the enormous expansion in Dutch foreign trade in general around 1600. The Flemings, who were driven north by the continuing war with Spain and growing religious persecution, brought with them considerable expertise, while the significance of foreign trade can be judged from the fact that as early as 1590 there appear to have been merchants from Haarlem and Amsterdam living in Poland, where much of the linen thread came from (flax spinning having greatly expanded as a rural industry in Silesia in the sixteenth century, however poorly paid). Also, the Netherlands used to be the international trading centre for Baltic potash, which was a major raw material in the bleaching process, being lixiviated to a lye and neutralized with sour milk, of which there was a plentiful supply from the dairy farms of North Holland.

By the beginning of the seventeenth century the industry was at its height and the bleacheries were treating not only local linen but also cloth imported from Flanders, Westphalia and France; this was then exported again to England, France, Portugal and Spain as "Holland"', "toile de Hollande", etc., thus providing a good example of an international trade cycle with, typically, the Dutch trader and entrepreneur at the centre. At this period in fact there were as many as twenty large establishments in the area, each employing 40 to 60 people, as well as a dozen or so smaller places. Many of the workers were women and many were migrants from places like Westphalia, Münsterland and Brabant, who flocked to Kennemerland in their hundreds in the spring at the start of the bleaching season. The pay was poor by local standards and the conditions in the bleaching works, which used a lot of chemicals and thus caused considerable water pollution, were not attractive.

By about 1650, however, the whole of the linen industry round Haarlem had already begun to decline, being siphoned away into the countryside where lower wages prevailed. The bleacheries still managed to keep going, particularly those producing better quality material, but with the establishment of new bleaching agents based on chlorine at the beginning of the nineteenth century, even they were forced to give up and move over to laundering.

■ This water-mill gives some idea of the type of mill that was still being used for papermaking in the mid-nineteenth century in the old-established industrial area of the Veluwezoom, on the eastern edge of the Veluwe plateau. The overshot wheel (i.e. a wheel turned by water falling from above) drives a heavy wooden camshaft which works large wooden drophammers inside the building. Under these hammers linen rags are reduced to a pulp which is subsequently fed to the "Hollander". This is an oval tub where the pulp is cut up even more finely by a revolving cylinder set with steel blades. The fibres are then scooped out of the tub on a fine copper-wire screen and allowed to strain. After straining, the resulting sheet is carefully lifted off, placed in a press between felt pads to absorb the remaining moisture, and finally hung up to dry in the vented loft. A business the size of this mill will not have employed many people, but there were many places much larger.

☐ The invention of printing at the end of the fifteenth century brought a considerable increase in the demand for paper, which up to then had been imported. Imported paper, however, was so expensive that people were soon trying to find ways of making it locally, and once again, as in the case of linen weaving (*cf.* p. 103), immigrants from the south played a major role. In fact they can be said to have set Dutch papermaking on its feet, since the technology they brought with them was virtually unknown in the north. (In this they clearly differed from the immigrant textile workers who, when they came, joined an existing industry).

At first attempts were made to set up mills elswhere in the country, probably in windmills, which at that stage were still not fully developed. But then, about 1600, attention turned to the Veluwe, which seemed to satisfy all the needs of this capital-intensive industry: pure water for the pulp, and also enough of it to power water-mills, which by that time had become well established in the region, so that there was an appreciable pool of experience to draw on. By 1650 there were as many as 28 paper mills in the area round Apeldoorn, and by 1740, when the industry was at its height, there were 174 of them on the Veluwe as a whole, quite apart from numerous other types of industrial water-mills.

screen

In the meantime, about 1670, producers had begun to show much greater interest in the better quality types of paper. This was particularly evident in the Zaan area to the north of Amsterdam, where windmills were used, and indeed by then the windmill had come into its own, being capable of virtually continuous production, with the result that it had become the universal engine for industrial processes. In the nineteenth century, however, most of these mills missed out on the next wave of industrial development (steam, improvements in mass production, etc.) and as a result all the paper mills in the Zaan area disappeared. Some of those on the Veluwe managed to carry on as laundries, but the irony of it is that the paper they had produced had been partly responsible – as the bearer of printed information – for the rapid scientific progress that led to the downfall of their traditional methods.

SAWMILL FROM NUMANSDORP (Z.H.)   47

■ This type of windmill – a Dutch invention dating from about 1600 – was specifically designed to saw imported logs into planks and ribs for building ships, houses, etc. The oldest parts of this particular mill, which is a fairly small example, probably date from about 1700. It was originally erected in Dordrecht but in 1854 it was moved to Numansdorp, where it remained in operation until it was brought to the museum. The moving of wooden mills and other wooden structures from one place to another used to be quite common.

cross-section
through mill

☐ Essentially the equipment consists of three saws mounted in vertical frames which were moved up and down by means of a crankshaft installed just below the windshaft (*i.e.* the axle of the sails). On the workfloor are a series of sleds, each of which held a log in position against the blade of one of the saws and carried it forward a step every time the saw was pulled upwards, so that the next downward stroke would bite into the wood again. To turn the sails into the wind, a winch was used to wind the whole body round, as in the case of the post mill (p. 97). In Dutch a mill like this is called a *paltrok* , which literally means a smock, but this should not be confused with the English name, smock mill, which is a wooden version of a tower mill (p. 99), where only the cap is turned.

The idea of the sawmill soon caught on. Medieval methods, using a long two-handed saw over a saw pit, were far too slow to keep up with the increasing demand ; so it is not surprising that there was a rush to invest in the new invention, even if it did mean an enormous capital outlay. As for the siting of the new mills, it must be remembered that the wood was largely pine and fir from the Baltic and was imported in cargo-boats based on ports like Hindeloopen (which partly owed its prosperity to the trade). Consequently, access to water was needed not only for steeping the new wood but also for reasons of transport; so the mills tended to be concentrated in areas with large tracts of water, like Amsterdam, the Zaan area to the north, and Dordrecht in the south, which were also old-established shipbuilding centres. Here they took their place amongst the hundred of other industrial windmills (for paint, paper, tobacco, spices, oil, etc.) that came to be such a feature of this part of the country in the seventeenth and eighteenth centuries. In the following century, however, the picture changed completely. Many of the mills went over to steam and some eventually expanded into large modern concerns. But there were many others that went out of business.

The most important buildings attached to a sawmill were the drying-sheds, where cut timber was left to dry, sometimes for years. There is one of these sheds, with sides open to the wind, in the museum (No. 126). This was built about 1850 and belonged to a sawmill attached to a timber and shipbuilding firm in Haarlem. It can only be viewed from the outside, as it is used as a store for building materials for the museum.

A fair-sized mill will have been run by a master, a foreman, a journeyman and several apprentices. In the "good old days", with a favourable wind, these will have worked all the hours there were, staying on after dark in wintertime and even sending one of the apprentices round the houses to collect their food so that they did not have to knock off for meals. Under these conditions, if they worked from five in the morning to eight or ten at night, eighty or so logs five to six metres long could probably have been reduced to planks.

SMALL DRAINAGE MILL 117
FROM WOUTERSWOUDE (Fr.)

■ This type of mill, known locally a *tjasker*, is a wind-driven adaptation of an Archimedes' screw. It is designed to pump water up out of low-lying waterlogged meadow-land into a wooden drainage gully which flows out on the other side of the dike. This example was built about 1870.

☐ The screw is encased in a hollow open-ended cylinder and is erected in a slanting position so that its foot is immersed in a small bowl-shaped reservoir into which, in the normal way, water from a whole grid of drainage channels would flow. The screw is directly driven by the sails mounted on the end of the shaft. When rotated, it raises the water up through the casing and spills it into the wooden gully. To stop the mill turning, there is a brake just behind the sails. This is a band brake, in which the band (gripe) acts on the rim of the brakewheel mounted on the shaft. A device like this is found in all mills but is not usually visible as it is mounted on the windshaft up in the cap. So that the mill can be pushed round into the wind, the frame (buck) which supports the shaft runs on rollers over a wooden rail. In actual practice both the rail and the wooden gully form a complete circle but only a section has been set up in the museum.
A small windmill of this type would only take about three weeks to build, and even simpler versions, worked by hand, were made too. Large numbers continued to be built right up until about 1930, most of them being made for farmers in Friesland, West Groningen, Drenthe and the northern part of Overijssel, who used them to drain their lowest meadows (usually 3 to 4 hectares, *i.e.* about 8 to 10 acres). In winter this land was normally left flooded and the mills were often wholly or partly dismantled and stacked away until the spring. Apart from farmers, however, peatmen also found a use for them in keeping down the level of ground water in the deep pits dug in the peat banks.

SMALL DRAINAGE MILL
FROM GORREDIJK (Fr.)

118

■ All the machinery in this mill, which was built in the
nineteenth century, is wooden. Like the *tjasker* (p. 109),
it has a screw mounted in a slanting position, with its foot
in the water. The casing here, however, is on the ground

and open at the top. The water which is pumped up flows over a low weir into a spillway on the other side of the dike.

☐ This type of mill is known as a hollow post mill. Both in construction and in the method of winding the sails into the wind, it is very similar to the conventional post mill (p. 97), but as its name suggests the post on which it rotates is not solid but hollow. Through this runs a wooden shaft which transmits the driving force of the wind on the sails to the gears connectd to the screw.

These mills were mainly found in Friesland and like the *tjasker* were mostly owned by farmers. They were more expensive and were not very powerful, but the running gear was more protected from the elements. Even so, they still had to be wound by hand and people sometimes had to come quite a long way to do it. However, there was a fantail version (No. 45) which hardly ever needed attention. This was because the large fantail mounted on the back of the rotating body ensured that the sails were always turned into the wind.

fantail-type mill
(No. 45)

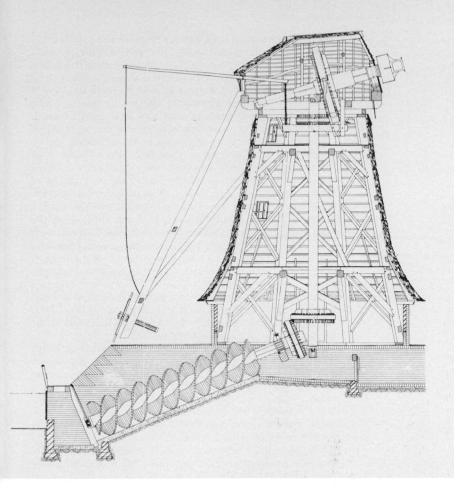

DRAINAGE MILL   48
FROM NOORDLAREN (Gr.)

■ This mill, which was built about 1862 and was used to
keep polder land drained, has a screw operated in the same
way as in the hollow post mill (p. 110) but the housing and
winding mechanism are different. It is in fact a wooden
version of a tower mill (p. 99), known as a smock mill (cf.
p. 107). In this particular instance, the wooden boards
which line the tapering octagonal framework are thatched
over, and so is the rotatable cap. It is capable of drawing
up to 50 or 60 cubic metres of water a minute and is a fine
example of drainage mill design of the type perfected by
the Dutch by about 1650.

☐ The windmill as such is not a Dutch invention and did not really begin to take a hold until about 1100. The earliest types were post mills for grinding corn (p. 97), and it seems that the earliest drainage mills also envolved from the post mill, possibly about 1400. Before then the low-lying areas in the north and west of the country had been continually affected by floods, which washed away large tracts of land. But after the first major attempts at building up the coastal defences at the beginning of the fourteenth century, it was possible to start reclaiming land by draining the lakes and meres. The first mills to work at all satisfactorily under these conditions were rather like the hollow post mills, though perhaps slightly larger and with paddle or bucket wheels instead of screws. With these considerable expertise and knowhow were built up and eventually this led to a period of intense activity between 1575 and 1650, when **the** great drainage mills of Holland were developed. Two engineers whose names are closely associated with this development were Jan Adriaansz. Leeghwater and Simon Stevin. But knowhow alone was not enough, of course. Capital and enormous enterprise were needed – and also available. To quote one example, reclamation of the Schermerpolder in North Holland, which was begun in 1631, needed 51 large mills drawing a total of 1000 cubic metres of water a minute over a period of four years before the ground was dry enough to be worked.

One of the problems with drainage mills is that their lifting power is limited, *i.e.* they cannot lift water above a certain height. To drain a lake and keep it dry, it was often necessary to raise the water up to four or five metres, which meant that a number of mills working in series had to be used. The diagram below shows how a series of three such mills with paddle wheels might operate. After 1650 the paddle wheel was gradually outsted in North Holland, Friesland and Groningen by the screw, and by the beginning of the nineteenth century steam pumps began to make their appearance; but it was still a long time before the highly efficient windmill was finally made redundant. The one in the museum, dating from 1862, is still exactly like the seventeenth-century mills, with only a few minor concessions to the "modern" steam age, such as a cast-iron windshaft for the sails.

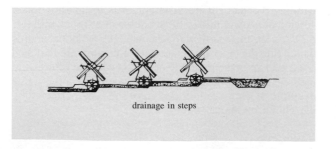

drainage in steps

It is difficult to appreciate the effect drainage mills have had on the appearance and agricultural economy of the western and northern parts of the country since 1600. Large lakes have been turned into rich farmland, boggy moorland has been turned into meadows, and weadows have been converted, by even better drainage, into highly profitable arable land. The reasons for this development were partly connected with the general expansion of trade and shipping and with the rising demand for raw materials by the new industrial mills that were going up in the west. As a result the farmers in the region acquired a modern approach to farming much sooner than their counterparts elsewhere (*cf.* pp. 67, 68 and 72): they were exploiting the land to satisfy national and international markets and were therefore only too ready to invest in dikes and drainage schemes. However, careful planning was also needed and this was put in the hands of specially instituted regional boards with very wide powers of control over dikes and bridges as well as waterways and drainage. For it was obvious that although dependence on the voluntary help of one's neighbours worked well on a small scale in villages and hamlets, this was not enough when it came to safe-guarding extensive tracts of fertile polder, sometimes several metres below sea level.

■ Herb have played an important part in daily life from earliest times. Around 800 Charlemagne promoted the cultivation of herbs in this country by, among other things, having a list drawn up of some seventy herbs that were to be grown in the imperial gardens. Most religious houses and hospitals in the Middle Ages and later also had herb gardens. As a result of the rise of the chemical industry and increasing importation from abroad the cultivation of herbs has suffered a sharp decline since the end of the last century.

☐ The herb garden of the Open-air Museum was opened in 1927 as an "Old Dutch Herb Garden", with the aim of providing information about herbs, their application and importance for doctor, apothecary, housewife and industry. Over 350 herbs and plants are to be found there in four sections: a monastery garden on the model of that designed in the 9th century for the monastery of Sankt Gallen in Switzerland; a section with medicinal herbs, which were employed in the past and some of which are still in use today (valerian, foxglove (*digitalis*), deadly nightshade (*belladonna*). A third section shows kitchen herbs and plants with industrial uses, *e.g.* for vegetable dyes (basil, chives, marjoram and hemp, flax, madder, woad, etc.), while in the last section are to be seen plants that played a role in folklore (herbs used in magic and witchraft). The entrances to the garden are marked by 18th-century gates. The stone pump in the Louis XIV style is one of the old parish pumps of Zwolle.

The building on the north side of the garden is a reconstruction of a herb drying-shed after an original at Noordwijk. Drying oven and workplace give an idea of the conversion of herbs into medicaments. In the exhibition room next door temporary exhibitions provide information about the cultivation, processing and application of herbs.

A detailed guide (in Dutch) to the herb garden of the Netherlands Open-air Museum is obtainable from the souvenir shop in the "Zaan district".

Top:
Restaurant ''De Oude
Bijenkorf''

Left:
Oil pitchers

Bottom left:
Stacking hay
in a Frisian barn

Bottom:
''Assendelft'' sideboard

Top left:
Dog churn

Top right:
Treshing with flails

Bottom:
Farm cart
from Kruiningen (Zld.)

Top:
Tilt at the ring (Zeeland)
in the museum

Top right:
Gig, about 1800 (North Holland)

Right:
Costume exhibition:
Palm Sunday (Northern Veluwe)

Bottom:
In the fowler's hut
from Aerdenhout (Z.H.)

Bottom right:
Bicycle, so-called Draisine, anno 1812